HESTER

HESTER

The story of
Mrs Hester Ann Rogers (née Roe)

An iconic figure from the 18th-century Evangelical Revival

CHURCH IN THE MARKET PLACE PUBLICATIONS
2011

Church in the Market Place Publications

British Library Cataloguing in Publication Data
A record for this book is available from the British Library

ISBN 978-1-899147-75-5

Typeset in Bookman Old Style
by Refinecatch Ltd, Bungay, Suffolk

Printed in Great Britain by
Cambrian Printers, Aberystwyth

Preface

When I first knew Methodism, a few years ago, an indescribable gloom had settled down upon us, raw, dreary, depressing as a London fog. Year after year we recorded a decrease in the number of our members. According to some, Methodism had done her work. We had developed to a very high degree the art of making ourselves miserable.[1]

The sentiments may sound familiar; but the article was written as long ago as 1883 by Hugh Price Hughes. In the same newspaper, the then President of Conference, Charles Garrett, urged his readers to gain inspiration by looking back to the early Methodists 'that we may be humbled and stimulated and so led to copy their example that we may be prepared to carry out and complete the work which they began'. Then specifically:

One of the great defects of the present generation of Methodists (that is in 1883) is their want to acquaintance with their Methodist forbears. There are, I fear, a large number of our young Methodists to whom the names of, say, John Nelson and Mrs Hester Ann Rogers have no charm. This ought not to be.[2]

By the time these words were written, Methodism had made its mark on British 19th-century society and any religious movement having as one of its principal objectives the saving of the collective soul of the nation would be justified in hailing infiltration into mainstream opinion as a victory, even if further battles lay ahead. However, success in terms of social acceptability brought its own perils and subsequent triumphs never seemed to match those of the pioneering days in terms of perceived drama and romance. 19th-century Evangelicals in general and Methodists in particular remained constantly aware that their roots lay in the Evangelical Revival of the 18th century and those of that period who had remained true to the Evangelical cause in the face of adversity achieved a status which had been denied them during their lifetime. The role models would come out of their number. From the world of literature, George Eliot provided them with a fictitious heroine in the character of Dinah Morris in her novel *Adam Bede*. In the plot, Dinah begins as an open-air preacher whose activism is ultimately curtailed by a combination of Methodist decree: 'Conference had forbid the women preaching' and limitations imposed on her by marriage and motherhood. 'She has given it up, all but talking to the people a bit in their houses.'[3] What 19th-century Methodists needed was an account of someone whose spiritual journey had taken them through a series of classic phases before reaching a triumphant destiny, beginning with an awareness of sin and ending with a 'good death'. For, in the words of Doreen Rosman, 'death beds had an almost sacramental function in evangelical experience'.[4]

In the key to the painting of the death bed of John Wesley by Marshall Claxton, exhibited at the Royal Academy in 1844, Hester Ann Rogers is kneeling by the side of the bed and is described as 'one of the saints of Methodism',[5] powerful evidence that projection of her life as a role model has been successful. Indeed, this was the objective of those who published the officially approved autobiography.

Vicki Tolar Burton suggests that Hester could have been chosen as a role model because she presented no challenge to the established male dominance within Methodism and her gift of spirituality could easily be contained within her limited role as mother and supportive wife of a full-time preacher. She illustrates this view in the sermon given by the Rev. Dr Thomas Coke when he took the trouble to mention that she did not preach.[6]

The point is fairly made and entirely consistent with what is otherwise known about Methodism at the beginning of the 19th century. Its leadership was politically conservative to the extent of being thoroughly reactionary, desperate to demonstrate its loyalty to the British Crown. As late as 1834 its secretary of Conference had declared 'we are to stand still, nor move in any direction'.[7]

Influential lay people particularly in the industrial north who were eager for political power were well aware that radical activities linked to Methodism would frustrate their ambition for Parliamentary representation. In their view this was no time to glorify assertive women.

Irrational but deeply engrained prejudice against women occupying Wesleyan Methodist pulpits or any other position of authority was endemic. A hundred years ago, Joseph Ritson ridiculed 19th-century Methodism by quoting the comment of a preacher conducting the funeral service of a departed President of the Wesleyan Conference: 'Balaam was converted by the preaching of an ass and Peter by the crowing of a cock and our lamented brother by the preaching of a woman; God often uses strange instruments.'[8]

So as someone who did not seek to break convention, Hester Rogers was accepted as an appropriate role model. Yet she was so much more than this and it is necessary to look for evidence that a late Victorian Methodist leader was justified in reviving memory of Hester, 'that her example might be followed'. If he was, then perhaps knowledge of her life, work and spiritual experiences might be of value to present and future generations. It is one purpose of this biography to investigate that possibility.

[1] *Joyful News*, first edition 22 February 1883, W.J. Tyne: Bacup, p. 1.
[2] Ibid., p. 3.
[3] George Eliot, *Adam Bede*, 1859, Collins: London, p. 563.
[4] Doreen Rosman, 'Faith and Family Life' in *Evangelicals and Culture*, 1984, Croom Helm: London, p. 132.
[5] Nehemiah Curnock (ed.), *The Journal of the Rev. John Wesley*, 1909, Robert Culley: London, vol. vii, p. 140 (hereafter *JWJ*).
[6] Vicki Tolar Burton, 'Re-reading *The Account of Hester Ann Rogers*', in Norma Virgoe (ed.), *Angels and Impudent Women*, 2007, Wesley Historical Society, pp. 52–68.
[7] Rev. Jabez Bunting, Wesleyan Conference, 1834.
[8] J. Ritson, *The Romance of Primitive Methodism*, 1909, Edward Dalton: London, p. 136.

Acknowledgements

Despite having been born and nurtured in Macclesfield, the name Hester Ann Roe meant nothing to me until I was well into my forties and accidentally came across her autobiography in a second-hand book shop. The first few words, 'I was born in Macclesfield in Cheshire, January 31st 1756,' were enough to launch me on a voyage of discovery which took many years and much research before I felt able to commit my findings to print in the form of this biography.

On this journey I have met many people who have been a source of inspiration and encouragement. In particular, I should mention the late Ron Clerk, history master supreme of Kings, Macclesfield, who taught a young pupil to be sceptical of recorded history and remained a neighbour and close friend for many years after school days were over; also the late Charles Legh, who was kind enough to share his considerable knowledge of Adlington Hall and the Legh family.

I am grateful to the archivists of all those institutions whose collections contain material relating to Hester, especially: Wesley's Chapel, London; Wesley College, Bristol; St John's College, Cambridge; and The John Rylands University Library, University of Manchester.

Finally, my thanks are due to Norma Virgoe of the Wesley Historical Society for her guidance and practical help in developing the final draft before publication.

Maccclesfield
2011

Chapter 1

Prior to Hester's Christian conversion, her lifestyle was scarcely that of a degenerate. J.D. Walsh observes that John Wesley 'noted how his preachers searching for flagrant sinners, unexpectedly picked up many devout folk'.[1] This was not growth frontal – by recruitment from the unchurched, but lateral – from committed church members. Hester clearly fell into this category.

Hester Ann Roe was the only daughter of the prime curate of St Michael's Church in Macclesfield, Cheshire, and she joined the Methodists in 1774 at the age of 18. In her diary, she faithfully recorded vivid accounts of her spiritual experience. These included an eye-witness account of the death of John Wesley who had been a personal friend and correspondent from the first time they met in 1776. All three thousand pages of this diary, in manuscript form, are held with other personal items in the John Rylands University Library, Manchester. This has never been published in full, although extracts, with 21 of her letters, a contribution from her husband and her funeral sermon, preached by the Rev. Dr Thomas Coke, were printed at intervals from 1796 and throughout the 19th century.

Andrew Worth, noting from the 1818 records of the Methodist Book Room that by then between 20,000 and 30,000 copies of Mrs Rogers' works had been sold, proposes the hypothesis that their selling power lay in the fact that 'they touched on matters to do with the soul that were beyond anything that Wesley's writings could offer'.[2] This claim can only be assessed within an understanding of evangelical spirituality, supporting the view of J.D. Walsh that the study of Evangelicalism is 'not for social historians only'.[3]

What Hester Rogers did and thought and the manner in which she expressed herself are of interest historically, but her importance as a Methodist depends on the extent to which she reveals the 'interior landscape of the experience of the heart' to quote Walsh's term.[4] Hester's own published testimony cannot simply be taken at face value. First her journal was written with the clear intention that it should be used as propaganda to encourage the faithful so that anything which might show the Methodists or Methodism in less than a favourable light was omitted and, second, those entrusted with the task of editing her writings for publication only selected those parts which they considered appropriate for tender and impressionable minds. In consequence, she emerges from the script as a prototype 19th-century Evangelical who meets all the standards expected by a society of which she knew nothing.

An examination of her unpublished letters and those sections of her journal that were never printed, gives a better understanding, not only of her, but also of the Methodism in which she was fully active. It also offers a fascinating insight into the ministry of the elderly John Wesley, preaching to the unconverted and at work among his flock.

Hester came to be both at the sharp end of Methodist evangelism and at the headquarters of its national operations. It is clear from her writings that she paid scant regard to the fundamental changes that were taking place in British society during her lifetime or indeed anything that was not directly related to the state of her soul or those of whom she sought to influence.

K. Gnanakan wisely observes that 'God chooses a particular people in a specific context to be the vehicle through which his purposes are to be accomplished.'[5] That truth could well be applied to individuals such as Hester. The dramatic sequence of events that resulted in her religious conversion and ultimate place of prominence in Methodism is closely linked with industrial and social revolution. She might have been oblivious to these changes, but those close to her, both her family and acquaintances, were not. They were heavily involved in the changing face of Britain with power to influence the destiny of the nation.

Chapter 2

By the time Hester was born on 31 January 1756, her father's brother, Charles Roe, was already well established as the leading entrepreneur in the Macclesfield textile and copper industries. Methodism had been present in the town since a brief visit by John Wesley on 10 May 1747, but its numbers were few and its influence small. Hester's father, James, was described by a contemporary as a 'likeable well-educated man of moderate attainments: he was tolerant but entirely conventional in his views'.[6]

The patron of the mother church at Prestbury was Mr Charles Legh of Adlington Hall, whose family chapel in St Michael's, Macclesfield, had been founded in 1422. The duties of patronage extended to Charles' wife, Hester, who became godmother to the infant Hester Roe who was, no doubt, named after her. The families were also linked historically and their heraldic shields were two of the 16 fixed to the outer walls of the tower of St Michael's in the 14th century.

Hester's father died shortly after her ninth birthday, leaving his widow, Elizabeth, Hester and six-year-old James. It is evident from her journal that for the rest of her life she valued the environment in which she was nurtured and the instruction her father had given her. He was a man of strict morals and piety who conducted 'constant family prayer'.[7] She records that by the age of five she 'took great delight in the Bible and could read any part of the Old or New Testament, always asking questions so as to obtain understanding of what I read'.[8] Supervision of her religious studies from this age took a disciplined form: 'My parents required that I should give an account every Sabbath evening of the sermons and lessons I heard at church and say my catechism to them, which they explained to my understanding.'[9]

Hester's tribute to her parents is not unconditional, in the tradition of all Evangelicals looking critically at their lives before their conversion experiences. Father's piety is credited as being 'as far as he was enlightened' and the lives of her parents are described as 'irreproachable' only as far as 'outward morality'.[10]

The reputation of the Hanoverian Anglican Church has been savaged by generations of historians who have experienced no difficulty in securing evidence of corruption, nepotism, immorality and neglected parishes. Dust may have settled on the Thirty Nine Articles as they lay on the shelves of many ecclesiastical residences, but not in the Roe household. James Roe took his job seriously, but was well aware of the low level of morality in society at large and was evidently anxious to influence his daughter against activities that he regarded as threats to her moral well being. Shortly before his death his advice was specific:

He warned me against reading novels and romances, would not suffer me to dance, nor go on visits to play with those of my own age. He said it was the ruin of youth to suppose they were only to spend their time on diversions.[11]

The advice presented young Hester with a problem that faced her throughout her formative years. Recognising that staying at home weeping with her grieving mother was hardly a healthy activity for a child, friends and relations invited Hester to their houses where she soon became a laughing stock among them for her 'seriousness and dislike to their manners and their plays'.[12] Their response was to persuade Mrs Roe to arrange for her daughter to take dancing lessons in order to raise her spirits and improve her 'carriage'.[13] The trouble was that this seemingly harmless and well-intentioned therapy was in direct conflict with the promises Hester had given to her dying father. She was quite able to enjoy herself as she indulged in what she was later to describe as this 'ensnaring folly',[14] but her guilt was deep seated and prompted frequent bouts of depression.

It is significant that the mature Hester, writing this part of her autobiography in the style of a confession, lays great emphasis on actions rather than beliefs; indeed matters of doctrine do not feature at all. James Roe did not tell his daughter what to believe, but how to behave in accordance with the lingering intellectual stance that based its faith on reason. Two elements of this were that the proper way to worship God was to practise virtue and that rewards and punishment would follow death.

We might now reasonably conclude that Hester's attempt to live a blameless life under the constant threat that damnation was a certain consequence of failure nearly ruined her childhood. Her Confirmation by the Bishop of Chester at the age of 13 ought to have been joyous occasion, but it was not.

> I resolved to attend that ordinance, though it was with many fears and much trembling for I believed till persons were confirmed, they were not alike accountable to God for their own conduct, but when this solemn renewal of the baptismal covenant was made in their own persons, then whosoever did not keep that covenant must perish everlastingly.[15]

The nearest she got to peace of mind was in looking round at other people who were 'guilty of things which my soul shuddered at',[16] and concluding that if she lived a 'tolerably moral life' God would pardon her 'through the merits of Christ' or at least she 'had as good a chance as others'.[17]

What were those sins that Hester believed put her immortal soul in peril? 'Anger, pride, disobedience to her mother, neglect of secret prayer and the reading of novels and romances.'[18]

Since 1775, theatre audiences watching Sheridan's *The Rivals* have been amused by Lydia Languish's instruction to her maid to 'Fling Peregrine Pickle under the toilet – throw Roderick Random into the closet – put the Innocent Adultery into the Whole Duty of Man and cram Ovid behind the bolster'.[19] Evidently it was a general problem at that time for mothers with daughters of an impressionable age. Hester might have been in danger of temporary mental impropriety but nothing worse. At least it gave her a break from living as though divine retribution was about to descend on her, which was more than she obtained from reading the religious books on offer with their monotonous stress on accountability. 'One of them asserted that we are all to be judged according to our works; therefore, if our good works are more than our evil ones, we are in a fair and sure way for heaven when we die, but if our evil works exceed our good, we may expect condemnation.'[20] This persuaded her to keep a written account of all her 'good' and 'bad' actions until the exercise stopped when the notebook dropped out of her pocket at a ball and prompted an outbreak of laughter at her expense.

The problem of linking piety to ethics on a personal basis was that it avoided any consideration of social evils or the conduct of others that seriously damaged the welfare of society as a whole. These were far more disturbing in nature and degree than anything Hester could recollect from her childhood. The malaise started at the top and worked its way down; 'The scandals of the Court were bad enough; but no Court, however bad, can compromise a nation. The mass of the population was coarse, insolent and cruel and permitted things which would not be tolerated for a moment now ... The general tone was low, violent and brutal.'[21]

18th-century diversions for the common people of Macclesfield included bear and badger baiting, cock fighting and joining the Market Day crowds to watch the criminals and vagrants being flogged, supporting the comment of H.D. Rack that 'Enlightenment thinking coexisted with barbarous punishments for crime and savage repression of the lower orders'.[22] Virtually all crimes of theft attracted the death penalty. As late as 1818, Ann Waterhouse, aged 16, was hanged for stealing silk to the value of a pound, public flogging in the Market Place continued until 1831 and in 1834, William Gee was transported for life for stealing a watch. William was 14 years old. Any husband tired of his wife's scolding had the option of curbing her speech by the fitting of an iron cage known as a 'brank' over her head or having her bound in a wooden ducking stool and ducked into the deepest part of the River Bollin under the aptly named Cuckstoolpit Hill. Both domestic punishments were regarded as hilarious spectator sports.[23]

How any of these so-called leisure activities were supposed to be consistent with a Christian faith based on ethics is not clear.

Chapter 3

After the death of her father, Hester and her mother were regular guests of the Legh family at Adlington Hall.

I was much beloved by my godmother, a lady of very considerable fortune and often spent most of the summer months at Adlington with her, where I was always treated as if she intended to bestow a handsome fortune on me. She introduced me into the company of persons in high life, and enabled me, by large presents, to dress in a manner suitable for such company.[24]

Adlington Hall is situated only four miles north of the town of Macclesfield, but in social terms it might well have been on another planet. When Charles Legh inherited the estate on the death of his father in 1739, the building had all the hallmarks of a Tudor manor house in the traditional 'black and white' Cheshire style. Over a period of 400 years, successive owners in the family succession had supervised the development of the property which had included the addition of the Great Hall at the end of the 15th century.[25] The most impressive feature of this hall is the organ, built by Bernard Smith with a completion date between 1660 and 1680. This instrument is of considerable historical importance in that only two other organs constructed by Smith have survived in their original state.[26]

Charles Legh carried out extensive alterations to the premises including the erection of a new wing, completed in 1757, incorporating a ballroom occupying the full length of the first floor.

Long before the days of planning committees, Charles Legh built an imposing Georgian wing complete with classical Greek portico on one side of his Tudor hall. This followed a fundamental change to St Michael's in 1739, when the spire was removed and the whole building, with the exception of the tower, demolished and replaced with a Georgian structure. In 1896 the church was rebuilt, with the exception of the tower, in a consistent gothic form.

The contribution of the Leghs of Adlington to culture went beyond the extension of their already impressive library collection and patronage of the arts to direct personal involvement. Elizabeth Legh, Charles' elder sister, had been an accomplished harpsichord player, taught by no less a music teacher than George Frederic Handel. After her death, the family's association with the celebrated Handel continued and he and Charles became firm friends.[27]

In the absence of guest lists recording the names of visitors in the 18th century, it is not possible to confirm by documentation the oral traditions that Handel stayed at Adlington on his way to Dublin for the first performance of his oratorio *Messiah* and that it was at Adlington that he composed the *Harmonious Blacksmith*. What is known for certain is that on his visit in 1751, he set to music a hunting song written by Charles Legh. The original autographed manuscript has been a treasured possession of the family ever since and remains on show.[28]

In looking back to her time spent at Adlington, Hester could only focus on her 'vanity and pride',[29] but there is reason for a more positive reflection on her life with the leisured classes at the height of the Enlightenment culture. The Adlington experience left its mark on her in that she acquired social and literary skills that would have been denied her had she stayed within the restricted environment of the town. In his tribute to her after her death, her husband made particular mention of her outstanding literary abilities.

> She had a critical knowledge of the English tongue and her application to reading from infancy made her capable of conversing upon any subject, whether of an historical, philosophical or theological nature.[30]

The prospects for this educated and highly intelligent young lady seemed excellent, despite her mother's concern, 'fearing the consequences of my living so much above my station in life'.[31] In fact, in the context of a British society that was undergoing change, it is difficult to determine just what Hester's 'station in life' was. As a daughter of a widowed mother, reliant upon family charity, she was not far up the social scale. However, Uncle Charles was a wealthy industrialist, firmly established in a middle class that was becoming increasingly powerful. Indeed, Hester might well have anticipated marriage to a prosperous member of the Cheshire set.

While at Adlington in the summer of 1773, she heard that her Uncle Roe had appointed someone to be a curate at St Michael's and that his choice had not met with universal approval. The curate in question 'was said to be a Methodist'[32] and the news was disturbing.

Chapter 4

As Hester Roe relaxed in the pleasant environment of Adlington in the summer of 1773, she could have had no idea that she would be a principal agent in the fundamental change in the religious scene, neither could she have anticipated that the decision of her uncle to nominate a particular young man as second curate at St Michael's would quickly bring confrontation between the Church establishment and a new middle class backed by the power of industrial wealth.

Charles Roe, Hester's uncle, was born at Castleton in Derbyshire on 7 May 1715, the son of the Rev. Thomas Roe, Vicar of Castleton and grandson of Robert Roe, lord of the manor of Hadley in Shropshire. His father died in 1723 and his mother in 1724 when he was only nine, the same year that his older brother, William, graduated from Oxford, took holy orders, and was made curate at Macclesfield until his death in 1730. Another older brother, James, the father of Hester Ann, graduated from Cambridge in 1732 and was presented to the living of Disley in 1733 before being appointed prime curate of Macclesfield in 1756, the year Hester was born. Research into the industrial career of Charles Roe was undertaken by Dr W.H. Challoner when preparing his article *Charles Roe of Macclesfield, 1715-81: An 18th-century Industrialist*[33] Dr Challoner was an eminent economic historian and he ranked Charles Roe as a great figure in the context of the earliest years of the Industrial Revolution.

Little is known about his early commercial activity except that in 1744 he was described as a 'button merchant', acting as an organiser and financier of the production and sale of buttons through a system based on domestic out-workers. This would have given him valuable experience in preparation for his first major industrial enterprise, the erecting a mill on Park Green, Macclesfield, for the throwing of raw silk by water power in 1743-4. In 1758, he diversified his business activities by building a copper works in partnership with Mr Rowland Atkinson, his brother-in-law and headmaster of the local grammar school. Expansion of his business was hampered by poor transport facilities and in 1766, a petition was presented to the House of Commons on behalf of Charles Roe and his associates for leave to build a canal linking Macclesfield to the River Weaver at Northwich with the prospect of navigation to Liverpool and development of his overseas trade. This project was frustrated by the Duke of Bridgewater in the House of Lords, anxious to preserve his own monopoly of inland water transport in the region. Roe responded by opening new works on the Mersey estuary.

The particulars of Charles Roe's business initiatives are not relevant to the story of his niece, Hester, but his character in later life, which was to a great degree fashioned by both his background and the manner in which he faced obstacles in his path, would be of crucial importance. Here was a man who had been orphaned at an early age and then been nurtured by his older brothers, two of whom were ordained into the Anglican Church. There is no record of his formal education, but having two Oxbridge brothers would be sufficient to guarantee a reasonable level of literacy. He had not been born into a wealthy family, but the Roe name was respectable enough and business could be developed through its many connections.

Asa Briggs makes the point that though 'the sense of station remained strong' there were 'extremely large numbers of middling folk, who increased in numbers and income during the 18th century.[34] Charles Roe was in the top layer of this level of society. He was a hard working, self-made man, with a good business brain. There were not too many people of his calibre in the 1740s and he prospered rapidly.

Charles Roe's family life had a far more direct relationship to religion in the town than to his business activities. He had a daughter and three sons by his first wife, Elizabeth, whom he married in 1743. She died in 1750 and, shortly afterwards, he married Mary Stockdale, who bore him a further eight children – five daughters and three sons in the ten years up to 1763. She died a month after her last confinement. Charles

Roe married his third wife, Rachel, in 1766 and they had one son, his thirteenth child. In the days of high infant mortality, it is remarkable that, even bearing in mind the Roe affluence, nearly all of them survived.

His second wife, Mary Stockdale, greatly influenced him in matters of religion and it was that lasting influence, long after her death, which affected decisions he had to make at critical times. He had first met her in London where she was a member of a Methodist society and he accompanied her to hear a number of prominent preachers, including the Wesley brothers. He was impressed and had these events taken place 50 years later, he would have had no difficulty in joining the Methodist church in his own town among the prosperous business leaders. But these were the early 1750s and it was made plain to the future Mrs Roe that there could be no way in which she could expect either her or her husband to associate with the local Methodist society. He was a successful businessman, the wealthiest burgess of the town, with a position in the community to uphold. The presence of either of them at the lowly Methodist preaching-house would be an embarrassment for all concerned.

The circumstances in which Mary Roe met John Wesley shortly before her death are not clear from his journal entry for 19 July 1764, but it confirms that Charles Roe was determined to keep her well away from Methodism.

> After preaching at Little Leigh I rode on to Macclesfield. Here I heard an agreeable account of Mrs Roe who was in the society at London from a child, but after she was married to a rich man durst not own a poor, despised people. Last year she broke through, and came to see me. A few words which I then spoke never left her, not even in the trying hour during the illness which came a few months after. All her conversion was then in heaven till, feeling her strength was quite exhausted, she said, with a smile, 'Death thou art welcome' and resigned her spirit.[35]

There is no reason to believe that the attitude of Charles Roe to Methodism ever mellowed; indeed, before long it was to harden into open hostility. Nevertheless he was not satisfied with the style of preaching he heard Sunday by Sunday at St Michael's and when the position of second curate became vacant in 1773, he decided to take action. Through his second wife's sister, he had become aware that a young ordained curate in Buckingham had been forced to leave his post for preaching the doctrines and in the style that Charles Roe found so attractive. In theory the appointment was by election of the municipal leaders. But Charles Roe's influence was quite enough to secure the appointment of the Rev. David Simpson who, according to intelligence reports received by Hester Roe in Adlington, 'was said to be a Methodist'.[36]

Chapter 5

David Simpson was born on 12 October 1745 at Ingleby Arncliffe near Northallerton, the son of a Yorkshire farmer. After preparatory education at local schools he entered St John's College, Cambridge, where he took degrees of BA in 1769 and MA in 1772. In a short biography written shortly after his death in 1799, the Rev. John Gaulter mentions that his principal interest when he entered university was 'mathematical science, which he cultivated with considerable success and had the fairest prospect of appearing in the first class of those who have attained eminence'.[37]

However, while at university, he came under evangelical influences and it is relevant that according to D.W. Bebbington, parts of the University of Cambridge later became something of an 'Evangelical citadel'.[38] After experiencing conversion at the age of 24, he was persuaded to transfer his studies to theology and was appointed curate at Ramsden in Essex, where he ministered successfully for two years before moving to Buckingham. His experience there was quite different for, according to his biographer:

> He was received without reverence or honour. He became a preacher of the doctrines of justification by faith and of the nature and necessity of a new birth unto righteousness, which was met by the hostility of the unsanctified clergy and the carnal and unchanged habits of men. An appeal was made to the Bishop for his removal who, after hearing both sides of the case, advised Mr Simpson that if he was determined to do his duty as a clergyman ought to do, then he must everywhere expect to meet with opposition.

Just at the time when his position in Buckingham became untenable, he received the invitation of Charles Roe to the post of second curate at Macclesfield.

There, in and out of the pulpit, he attacked sin in its most heinous forms or more imposing delusion, He enforced the doctrine of pardon through faith in the blood of the covenant and the fruits and witness of the Spirit.[39]

It is fortunate that David Simpson published the scripts of many of the sermons he preached in the first year of his ministry at St Michael's so that the summary of the substance of his preaching given in Gaulter's biography can be tested. First of all, here he is in full cry on the subject of Biblical authority:

... the Bible is the word of God ... We ought to be ruled and governed by it here ... we must be tried and judged by it at our last day, consequently it is of infinite and everlasting importance to every soul of us ... There is no principle peculiar to a Churchman, Methodist or Dissenter, 'tis a principle common to them all. They are all agreed in this fundamental point, the Bible is the Word of God: by its decision we must stand or fall. O that we could prevail with you, my brethren, to set about reading the Bible with a becoming seriousness and attention: sin would flee before you and we should see Satan fall from heaven as lightning. It is the devil's artifice to keep the Bible from the common people. He knows, he well knows, that his kingdom cannot stand if mankind in general could be prevailed upon to study and regard the sacred writings. O, therefore, get Bibles, young and old get Bibles. Read them with humble, earnest prayer to God for the enlightening influences of his Holy Spirit to enable you to understand them. Read to practise, read to obey. Read to mend the heart, not merely fill the head.[40]

Having made plain his conviction in biblical authority, he then uses a biblical example to illustrate that doctrine which proved to be so unacceptable to the parishioners of Buckingham – justification by faith:

The thief upon the cross had been notorious for his villainies. He had transgressed, not only the laws of his God, but also the laws of his country, insomuch that public justice demanded satisfaction. He was apprehended, arraigned at the bar, found guilty, and condemned to be crucified. As he hung bleeding upon the cross he cries out to Jesus, 'Lord remember me when thou comest into thy kingdom.' What answer does the expiring Saviour make? 'Today' he says, 'shalt thou be with me in Paradise.' Now the criminal was either saved or he was not saved. If he was not saved, the words of Jesus were false: if he was saved, it was either by faith or works: and if he had no boasted good works to produce, as from the circumstances of the story it appears he had not, then he must have been justified and saved by faith alone in Jesus, the Redeemer. Faith was the instrument, the death of Jesus alone was the meritorious cause of his salvation.[41]

Just in case any of his congregation in Macclesfield could have been tempted to think that his experience in Buckingham might have taught him to tone down his preaching on the twin themes of justification and spiritual renewal, his proclamation is uncompromising.

Another objection … with bigoted narrow-minded people is that 'none but the Methodists and enthusiasts preach up the necessity of being regenerate and born again' … To this it is answered: If the doctrine is not a doctrine of reason and scripture, let it be given up. But if it is, we are bold to contend for it, though all the world should call us enthusiasts. Party names and ill-natured distinctions are with us of very small weight.

There is no evidence that during the first year of his ministry in Macclesfield, David Simpson had any connection with the Methodists. He simply acknowledged that he shared a common belief with them in certain doctrines that he advocated from his pulpit with powerful conviction. Nevertheless, it was a fact of life that Methodism was not held in high esteem by the majority of David Simpson's congregation at that time, and sermons of that nature were bound to divide opinion.

Robert Roe, son of Mary Roe (née Stockdale), was only eight years old when his mother died so it was not likely that her Methodist background would have had any lasting effect on him. Consequently, when he returned home from Manchester Grammar School for a vacation, the changes brought about to the social life of his family through the influence of David Simpson, were less than welcome.

> I was filled with grief and amazement to find that Mr Simpson had turned all things upside down. Every pleasure my heart was set upon was refused me by my father and his present wife, as being contrary to the will of God. Our nightly dancing with the young people of the town was broken up; my sisters were as grave as old women. This was more than I had resolution to bear and being countenanced by many of my pretended friends I abused Mr Simpson, blamed my parents and endeavoured with all my might to bring them over again to their wonted gaiety. Yet my conscience often constrained me to acknowledge Mr Simpson to be a candid, pious man, one that desired to do what was right, though my prejudices made me account him an enthusiast.[42]

At Adlington, Hester Roe was coming to the end of her summer visit and particular news about David Simpson concerned her:

> I heard also that this new Clergyman preached against all my favourite diversions, such as going to plays, reading novels, attending balls, assemblies, card tables etc. But I resolved he should not make a convert of me, and that if I found him, on my return home, such as was represented, I would not go often to hear him.[43]

Chapter 6

The trouble for Hester when she first heard the sermons of the Rev. David Simpson had nothing whatever to do with the social acceptability of Methodism but the fact that he raised the spirit of her dead father within her conscience. When his sermons were published in 1774, David Simpson had not reached his 30th birthday but he was worldly-wise. After leaving the security of home and village life in rural Yorkshire, he had spent his undergraduate years in Cambridge with the sons of the aristocracy and landed gentry. He was appalled at their lack of moral standards and his indignation about the state of society at large shouts from the pages of the scripts of his sermons. He not only despised the immorality of the aristocracy, he loathed the trappings of wealth that he regarded as the manifestations of corruption.

> Let them the gay unthinking sons and daughters of pleasure content themselves with their tinsel and their plumes; let them enjoy the things of sense and time; let them neglect and despise a little longer the sublime delights of righteousness, peace and joy in the Holy Ghost. We know that God is not mocked and whatever a man sows, he shall also reap; he that sows to the flesh shall of the flesh reap corruption.[44]

The 17-year-old Hester was perplexed. In her limited world, moral and ethical behaviour was a personal matter linked to ultimate judgment; it had nothing whatsoever to do with the style of dress. The sermons contained a specific message of the offer of salvation through Christ, but they also emphasised the fallen nature of humanity and that was upsetting.

What they also did was to reject any concept of a universal redemption rendering faith irrelevant; a possibility she had relied on as a last resort of comfort.

Hester

David Simpson presented the argument:

> God is merciful. He is so good, so amiable, so gracious
> and benevolent a being that he will never damn his
> creatures for the enjoyment of a little forbidden pleasure
> sometimes. Besides Jesus Christ hath died for mankind;
> we are all imperfect creatures; God has made us with
> propensities of various kinds; and why, if not to be
> indulged? And, after all, if there should be any harm,
> there is time enough hereafter to repent and amend.

Then he crushed it:

> if you harden your neck and live in contempt both of
> divine and human laws your case is desperate. You will
> live pitied and despised by the virtuous and good; and
> you will die in disgrace; you will rise in shame; you will
> be struck with ten-fold confusion before the bar of
> God.[45]

A young lady with a skeleton of guilt in her psychological
cupboard could not cope with this tirade. David Simpson was
concerned about far more than a girl disobeying a single
parent, but this did not matter to Hester.

> Mr Simpson's sermons began to sink more deeply into
> my heart. So great was my obstinacy and folly that I
> would come out of the church weeping, and with the
> next person I met would ridicule the sermon that
> affected me: lest I should be thought or called a
> Methodist![46]

Whatever conclusion Hester might have retained from her
pleasant surroundings and social contacts at Adlington was
brutally condemned.

> Riches and ease beget luxury. Luxury begets
> debauchery and degeneracy of manners. Debauchery
> and degeneracy of manners beget divine judgments. And

divine judgments beget among mankind, weeping and mourning, lamentation and woe.[47]

Hester responded by searching the whole of Scripture to find any reference that might justify dancing for pleasure. Apart from the dancing of the daughter of Herodias, which was the 'cause of the beheading of a servant of God',[48] she could only find the records of Miriam and David dancing, but these were part of acts of worship. This exercise prompted only further repression and guilt; 'Therefore, I stifled these convictions with all my might; and after this, ran more eagerly than ever into all pleasurable follies.'[49]

Even seemingly harmless and edifying reading could not end her depression.

I went through several English and Roman histories; Rollin's Ancient History and Stackhouse's History of the Bible, intending to go through the Universal History also. And I now believed myself far wiser than any person of my age.

To Hester, improvement of the mind brought only an awareness of 'the sin of pride'.[50] In her autobiography, Hester makes a specific reference to having been greatly affected when David Simpson preached on the re-birth of a Christian from John 3:3 in January 1774. 'I saw and felt that I must experience that divine change or perish.'[51] From the script of the sermon, it is hardly surprising that Hester gained the impression that he was preaching to her personally.

We see such strange inconsistent characters among Christians. Sometimes they have all the appearance of being good and religious: at other times you'll observe them quite contrary. There is no consistence or uniformity in their religious conduct. Sometimes they'll put on a sanctified countenance, come to Church and Sacrament and you would conclude they are about to commence very pious. But wait a little and you shall see them acting their part in very different scenes: gay, giddy, thoughtless; pursuing the wanton delights of

Bacchus and Venus, or squandering their golden hours at balls, assemblies or card tables. Strange inconsistent characters indeed![52]

Three months later, on Palm Sunday, David Simpson developed his attack on sin in his parishioners into what amounted to a personal interrogation from the pulpit; 'Have you renounced the devil and his works, the pomps and vanities of this wicked world with every sinful desire? Have you never set up idols in your heart? Now, what think you of the state of your souls before God?'[53]

She could only judge herself to be guilty on all counts and to the impressionable Hester, the evidence that confirmed her guilt was hanging in her wardrobe:

I slept not that night: but arose early next morning and, without telling my mother, took all my finery ... and ripped them all up, so that I could wear them no more. I then cut my hair short that it might not be in my own power to have it dressed; and in the most solemn manner, vowed never to dance again.[54]

It is hardly surprising that Hester did not find peace of mind out of an act of destruction. She had simply responded to the impassioned pleas of a fervent preacher who linked spiritual health to a puritan lifestyle. In her autobiography she records her state of mind; 'It had been well for me if I had then known the Methodists, but I had none to instruct me.'[55]

David Simpson had taken her to the point of longing for an 'experience of divine change'[56] but he could not go beyond this. This simple acknowledgement of a doctrinal truth was something she had always taken for granted. She needed more than this.

Shortly afterwards, a rebellious and confused Hester, finding no answer elsewhere, visited the Methodist preaching house at five o'clock one morning on the advice of a neighbour, who had assured her that the Methodists 'had been the means of great blessings to his soul'.[57]

Mr Samuel Bardsley preached from 'Comfort ye, comfort ye my people, saith your God'. I thought every word was for me. He spoke to my heart as if he had known all the secret workings there; and pointed all such sinners, as I felt myself to be, to Jesus crucified. I was much comforted; my prejudices were now fully removed, and I received a full and clear conviction: 'These are the people of God, and show, in truth, the way to salvation.'[58]

Chapter 7

Hester Roe attended the early morning service at the preaching house just one month after a visit by John Wesley, an event that had been of considerable significance for the local Methodists. On Easter Sunday, 3 April 1774, they celebrated the appointment of the first Methodist Mayor of the Borough and John Wesley was determined to join the mayor's procession to St Michael's. The journey to Macclesfield was not without its difficulty:

Wednesday 30 March.
I went to Congleton, where I received letters informing me that my presence was necessary at Bristol. So about one I took a chaise and reached Bristol about half an hour after one the next day. Having done my business in about two hours, on Friday in the afternoon, I reached Congleton again (about 140 miles from Bristol), no more tired (blessed be to God) than when I left it.[59]

Wesley preached at Congleton in the evening of Good Friday and at five o'clock on the mornings of Saturday and Sunday, before travelling the eight miles to Macclesfield. After this punishing schedule, he 'came just in time to walk to the old church with the mayor and two ministers'.[60] This was the first occasion on which Wesley met David Simpson.

By 1774 Macclesfield Methodism had made considerable progress since its origins in the 1740s when a Mary Aldersley held meetings for prayer, bible reading and religious conversation in her cottage, Shrigley Fold, in the hills to the east of the town on the Derbyshire border. In those days, any group of this kind was likely to be labelled 'Methodist' and the occasional visit of the itinerant preacher, John Bennet of Chinley, known then as the 'Macclesfield and Sheffield Carrier', soon established Shrigley Fold as being on 'John Bennet's Round'. In his journal John Wesley records that on the 26 and 27 April 1745, at John Bennet's request, he 'preached at several places in Lancashire and Cheshire'.[61] A footnote refers to Mary Aldersley having 'brought information from another preaching at which she had been that Mr Wesley would preach at Roger Moss's near Rode Hall'.[62]

There follows an account by Thomas Buckley of Astbury, of the visit by John Wesley and three other preachers:

> When night came six or seven of us went. My wife carried a child, which was eight months old, in her apron. When we arrived, there was Mr Wesley and three more preachers. Mr Wesley preached from Romans 3:23, 'For all have sinned and come short of the glory of God.' He gave notice for preaching at five o'clock on the following morning. We got leave of Roger Moss to sit by the fire all night. We brought some little books to read. When preaching was over, we returned, well pleased with our journey. Mr Wesley gave notice for preaching at the end of the month. We all resolved to go, which we did.[63]

When John Wesley next visited the area in November 1745, his planned itinerary had to take into account that the rebel army of Charles Edward Stuart (Bonnie Prince Charlie) was marching south to Derby and Wesley was less impressed by those 'those poor tools of watchmen who stood, with great solemnity, at the end of almost every village'.[64] On Friday 8 November:

> Understanding that a neighbouring gentleman, Dr C., had affirmed to many that Mr Wesley was now with the Pretender, near Edinburgh, I wrote him a few lines. It may be he will have a little more regard to truth or shame, for the time to come.[65]

In 1746 the Shrigley Fold meeting attracted an illiterate tailor, George Pearson, and in the spring of the following year, he heard that both John Wesley and John Nelson would be preaching in Manchester. He walked the return journey of 36 miles and invited Wesley to preach outside his home on

Waters Green, Macclesfield, when he was next in the district. John Wesley accepted the invitation and the visit on Sunday 10 May 1747 was recorded in the journal.[66]

After preaching, John Wesley appointed George Pearson as a class leader with the instruction to secure at least twelve members with the promise of a further visit. This illustrates Wesley's pragmatic approach to evangelism. In fact he did not see George Pearson again for another twelve years, but the roots of George's Methodism were firmly established in the Shrigley Fold fellowship and did not depend on occasional visits by itinerant preachers.

Once George Pearson had recruited his first four class members they needed somewhere to worship together in the town and rented an outbuilding formerly used as a stable. 'Such meanness of accommodation was not unknown in the annals of Christianity,'[67] observes Benjamin Smith and 'when they had a preacher, and the weather proved favourable, there was abundance of room outside'.[68]

These were early days in terms of Methodist organisation on a national scale and as Macclesfield was in the 'York Round' comprising the six counties of Yorkshire, Cheshire, Lancashire, Derbyshire, Nottinghamshire and Lincolnshire, they did not have to worry about inclement weather too frequently; the old stable was usually quite big enough. Progress was slow, but among the new members soon after 1747 was Mrs Elizabeth Clulow, the wife of a local baker.

By 1750, membership of the society had outgrown the humble stable, but they had no resources from which to build their own premises and if a cottage were bought without declaring the nature of the occupancy they would be exposed to legal eviction. The solution was for a cottage to be leased for a period of 40 years in the joint names of George Pearson and Elizabeth Clulow. To increase its capacity, half the ground floor ceiling was removed to create a balcony facing the pulpit.

When John Wesley wrote of the Methodists being 'poor despised people', he was referring to the early years of Mary Stockdale's married life with Charles Roe in the 1750s, but this description would not have been appropriate if related to the time of the journal entry in 1764. Although the original Methodists in Macclesfield had been humble people, by then, members of prosperous families involved with commerce and industry had joined the society, including the Ryles and Daintrys. A young John Ryle had already accumulated sufficient wealth to provide a site for a new meeting-house and the membership as a whole had little difficulty in raising money to complete the building project. Indeed, by 1774, practically every factory owner except Charles Roe was a Methodist and the Macclesfield Methodists had emerged as leaders in the earliest days of the Industrial Revolution.

By the time Hester Roe attended the service in May 1774, the Methodists were already planning a move to a substantial chapel nearer to the centre of the town.

George Pearson remained illiterate throughout his long life, but his two sons were educated, built factories and became mayors of the Borough. On his death, John Ryle, that first Methodist mayor, left his son over a quarter of a million pounds. Two of Mrs Clulow's sons became lawyers; John was appointed Town Clerk and William set up his own practice in Chancery Lane, London, where he acted as a legal consultant to John Wesley. It was William Clulow who drew up John Wesley's Will that Elizabeth Clulow signed as one of the witnesses, and the Deed of Declaration, which established the legal status of Methodism prior to Wesley's death.

Each of these families founded what can only be described as ecclesiastical dynasties. George Pearson's granddaughter, Esther, married the Rev. John Bowers, an early President of Conference after Wesley's death. John Ryle's grandson, J.C. Ryle, was the leading Evangelical Anglican in the second half of the 19th century and was appointed the first Bishop of Liverpool. J.C. Ryle's son, Herbert, became Bishop of Winchester, before being promoted as Dean of Westminster in 1911. Elizabeth Clulow's granddaughter, also named Elizabeth, was the mother of John Rigg, the second Principal of Westminster Training College.

In 1787 John Wesley expressed his concern about the possible effect of all this accumulated wealth on the spiritual well being of the members of his society.

Saturday 31 March
I went on to Macclesfield, a people still alive to God, in spite of swiftly increasing riches. If they continue so, it will be the only instance I have known in above half a century. I warned them in the strongest terms I could and believe some of them had ears to hear.[69]

So the Methodists of 1774 were spiritual, industrious, resourceful, committed and ambitious, but none of these positive characteristics found favour with the Roe family once they heard about Hester's presence at the five o'clock service.

Chapter 8

When Hester's mother heard of her daughter's attendance at the meeting house, she would have turned her out into the street but for the intervention of Uncle Charles Roe. As it was, she was confined to her room for eight weeks on a diet of bread and water during which time she was urged to end her association with the Methodists, a state of affairs noted by the bewildered Robert Roe on his Whitsun vacation. 'My cousin Roe, formerly my chief companion, under strong convictions and greatly persecuted.'[70]

A summer spent at Adlington Hall did nothing to change her resolve:

I left all company many times in a day to retire in secret. I refused to conform in dress, or in anything my conscience disapproved; and when called upon gave reasons for my conduct as the Lord enabled me; but always with meekness and often with tears of self-abasement; so that in a little time, finding all their efforts in vain, they began to let me alone.[71]

On their return home at the end of October, Hester informed her mother that she would sooner leave and enter service elsewhere than be separated from her Methodist friends, but proposed that as an alternative, she would prefer to act in the role of a servant in her own house. After consulting a number of friends and after pressure from her brother-in-law, Charles, Mrs Roe consented, convinced that Hester, 'who has never been accustomed to hard labour, would soon be weary and give it up'.[72] On 1 November 1784, she entered upon her 'new employments joyfully', to use her own words.[73]

The actions of his niece must have placed Charles Roe in a position of some difficulty. He may have intervened simply out of a concern for her welfare in the hope that her temporary religious obsession would fade with the passing of time. This was a patriarchal society and she was his only niece, reliant on his charity. Denied access to her mother's home, Hester would have had to seek an appointment as a maid or governess in the household of a family with which he would probably have had business associations. Furthermore, virtually all the other successful businessmen in the town at that time were Methodists. His intervention was inconsistent with his later treatment of his own sons, but consistency was never a feature of Charles Roe's relationship with Evangelicalism.

The reaction of Mrs Hester Legh to her goddaughter's conduct was entirely hostile, but it should be acknowledged that the landed gentlefolk of Cheshire had good reason to be suspicious of Methodist practices. Hester records that her initial prejudice against Methodism was based on stories she had heard as a child.

> I was fully persuaded that to be a Methodist was to be all that is vile under the mask of piety. I believed their teachers were the false prophets spoken of in Scripture, that they deceived the illiterate and were little better than common pickpockets; that they filled some of their hearers with despair, that they had dark meetings and pretended to cast out devils, with many other things equally false and absurd, but all of which I believed.[74]

'False and absurd' these accusations might have been in relation to the highly respectable Methodists in Macclesfield in 1774, but Methodism beyond the control of the disciplined leaders in the industrial towns had attracted groups of people whose beliefs were far from conventional and who manifested their spiritual ecstasy in quite extraordinary ways. For example, the 'Magic Methodists of Delamere Forest' conducted their strange rituals which involved falling into trances or 'visions',[75] scarcely 20 miles from Adlington and even if the Leghs had no immediate knowledge of their practices, their friends in rural mid-Cheshire most certainly would. Exaggerated tales no doubt reached the ears of those guardians of conventional religion, but as late as 1786 and as near to Macclesfield as Chapel-en-le-Frith, just over the Derbyshire border, John Wesley had reason to be concerned about the behaviour of members of his own society.

> Even when they are full of love, Satan strives to push many of them to extravagance. This appears in several instances: - Frequently, three or four, yea 10 or 12, pray aloud all together. Some of them, perhaps many, scream all together as loud as they possibly can. Some of them use improper, yea indecent, expression in prayer. Several drop down dead; and are stiff as a corpse, but in a while they start up and cry 'Glory! Glory! Perhaps 20 times together. Just so do the French prophets and, very lately, the Jumpers in Wales[76], bring the real work into contempt. Yet, whenever we reprove them, it should be in the most mild and gentle manner possible.[77]

Much earlier, in March 1762, the Macclesfield Methodists had experienced a revival in their meeting room under the preaching of John Oldham, following a visit to the area of the fervent evangelist, John Furz. The meeting, beginning on a Monday evening, lasted until six o'clock the following morning, when members went to work, and further revival meetings, quite unplanned and without the presence of an itinerant preacher, took place each evening for the rest of the week. To Benjamin Smith, the ordained Methodist historian, this was the Holy Spirit visiting his people.

> The loud and bitter cry, arising from many sinners pricked to the heart, was heard afar and it was prolonged. Again and again the holy song or shout of gladness arose, as another and another soul stepped into the liberty of God's 'dear children' and again and again the cry of many was lifted up on behalf of those who still remained in bondage.[78]

The cries were not only 'heard afar', they also reached the ears of the Rev. James Roe up the hill at St Michael's and in time his disapproval would be expressed to his young daughter, Hester Ann, then an alert six-year-old.

In the 18th century, attitudes to religious revivals fell into two quite distinct categories. Not everyone agreed with Benjamin Smith as Gail Malmgreen observes: 'Critical contemporaries were inclined to see the effervescence of spirituality as the outbreak of vulgar "enthusiasm".[79]

Polite society did not approve of such excesses of the kind recorded in the 'mad Methodist magazines, full of miracles and apparitions, of preternatural warnings, ominous dreams and frenzied fanaticism'.[80]

It was not likely that Mrs Legh saw the Methodism with which her goddaughter was associated as a social or political threat; she was probably more worried about her sanity. However, British society in 1774 was established on strictly hierarchical lines and any move to cross those boundaries was discouraged, particularly by those in authority who simply wanted to maintain the *status quo*

The Legh dynasty had been under threat on more than one occasion, usually by backing the losing side in times of armed conflict. One ancestor had been beheaded on the orders of Bolingbroke, later Henry IV, after defending Chester on behalf of Richard II and it had actively supported Charles I against the forces of Cromwell. The restoration of Charles II had been welcomed, but as the Leghs had subsequently supported the monarchy of James II, his flight to France and the accession of William and Mary was scarcely a series of events to be celebrated. By 1745 any enthusiasm to back another Jacobite cause had long since waned and there was never any question of the Leghs welcoming Bonnie Prince Charlie and his odd assortment of warriors when they decided to loot Adlington Hall in the course of their ill-fated journey from Derby.

English social and political life was stable and comfortable and although 'early Methodist preachers did not mince their words in attacking the ecclesiastical and social hierarchy',[81] it is not likely that the Methodist inclinations of a teenage goddaughter caused undue alarm. The threat to ecclesiastical, social and political control would come from elsewhere and it would come soon.

Chapter 9

Methodists of the 18th century 'believed conversion to be an essential and central spiritual experience that made a person a Christian when she had renounced her sins, escaping the pains of hell and had accepted Christ in faith, thereby obtaining the promise of salvation'.[82]

This concept of justification by faith was grounded in the Epistles of St Paul, emphasised by Martin Luther at the time of the Reformation and preached from church pulpits and in the open air throughout the Evangelical Revival. To the Evangelicals, it was far more than an important element of theology, it was an experience 'often ardently sought, for others as well as for oneself'[83] and something Hester was already eager to achieve when attending to her household duties.

At this time, Hester was constantly under three influences, the weekly sermons of David Simpson, the fervent preaching of the Methodists and tracts and sermons written and published by John Wesley.

All students of evangelical history will readily agree with H.D. Rack that 'Sermons are always more or less cold and formal in print, and it is particularly difficult to reconstruct the manner and effects of a revivalist preacher when one has only the apparently dull discourses surviving in print.[84] The sermons of David Simpson are the exceptions that prove the rule. His sermon of the Atonement, based on the text of Psalm 85: 10 – 'Mercy and Truth are met together: Righteousness and Peace have kissed each other' explains the condition of humanity. 'The whole New Testament turns upon this hinge. It supposes us to be lost, undone, ruined, guilty, fallen creatures.'

His sermon was carefully argued and movingly urged and reached its climax with the plea:

'What shall be the end of those who obey not the Gospel of Christ? O the misery and unhappiness of that man, who rejects this last, best gift of God to a guilty world! Good had it been for him, if he had never been born!' Surely my brethren, none of you are in that wretched number. O if you die, you die from between the extended Arms of Mercy! You die surrounded with streams of salvation.[85] Forgive me, O Christians, for speaking with so much warmth and earnestness upon this pleasing theme. 'Tis a matter of infinite importance. Let sceptres, crowns and kingdoms be neglected, but I beseech you neglect not the Gospel Salvation.

O that I had the zeal of a Paul and the eloquence of an Apollos: O that I had an angel's voice and seraph's fire to pierce and enter and take possession of your souls; then, would I compel you to come in and partake of rich, redeeming Love![86]

If David Simpson was pushing Hester to an experience of conversion, then the Methodists were pulling her, both in the heady atmosphere of their worship and in the weekly class meetings, the system of John Wesley for building up the faith of those who had been awakened by preaching. This term 'awakened by preaching' is significant for Methodism made no requirement of belief of those attending its classes, so that membership was freely open to those who were not Christians, committed or otherwise. In this intimate and supportive atmosphere of the class, members were encouraged to reveal matters that concerned them and to share religious experiences with others.

In his detailed study of class meetings in early Methodism, D.L. Watson identifies religious experience as the critical element that John Wesley added to 'the Anglican theological method of scripture, tradition and reason'[87] in organising his classes. This concept of religious experience went right back to the origins of Methodism and lack of conviction in John Wesley's answer to the Moravians when he was questioned about his personal assurance of salvation:

'... but do you know He has saved you?' I answered, 'I hope He has died to save me.' He only added, 'Do you know yourself?' I said, 'I do.' But I fear they were vain words.[88]

This was precisely the spiritual state of Hester Roe when she first associated with the Methodists. She needed no lessons in matters concerning Anglican doctrine, but Wesley's class leaders not only had religious experience in depth, but they were also well practised in nurturing new members.

It is possible to gauge the value Hester placed on her membership of a class from a letter to a friend on 10 December 1776. 'I believe I shall have reason to bless God to all eternity that I ever joined the Methodists.'[89]

Hester was a voracious reader and thought nothing of tackling at least 400 pages of quarto each day during intervals in the course of her domestic duties. This included all Wesley's printed works and, not surprisingly, bearing in mind the content of the sermons of David Simpson she heard in church, she paid particular attention to his sermon on Justification. 'This sermon I read many times over with prayer, and could sometimes almost embrace the promises.'[90] The promises in Wesley's sermon were very specific:

> The plain scriptural notion of justification is pardon, the forgiveness of sins.[91] Justifying faith implies not only a divine evidence or conviction that 'God was in Christ reconciling the work unto Himself' but a sure trust and confidence that Christ died for my sins, that He loved me and gave Himself for me.[92]

It ends with an impassioned plea to the reader:

> Who art thou that now seest and feelest both this inward and outward ungodliness? Thou art the man! I want thee for my Lord! I challenge thee for a child of God by faith! The Lord hath need of thee. Thou who feelest thou are just fit for hell are just fit to advance His glory; the glory of his free grace, justifying the ungodly and him that worketh not. O come quickly! Believe in

the Lord Jesus Christ, and thou, even thou, art reconciled to God.[93]

D.W. Bebbington observes that Methodists 'usually looked for a datable crisis', though equally they expected it to be preceded by a long period of 'awakening'.[94] In Hester's case, her 'awakening' had lasted six months within the Methodist fellowship and culminated in a night of intense struggle before the moment of spiritual release came.

Then did he appear to my salvation. In that moment my fetters were broken, my hands were loosed and my soul set at liberty. The love of God was shed abroad in my heart and I rejoiced with joy unspeakable. Now if I had possessed 10,000 souls I could have ventured them all with my Jesus. I would have given them all to him! ... My sins were gone, my soul was happy and longed to depart and be with Jesus. I was truly a new creature: and seemed to be in a new world. I could do nothing but love and praise my God; and could not refrain from continually repeating, 'Thou art my Father! O God, thou art my God' while tears of joy ran down my cheeks.[95]

Chapter 10

Hester was released from her domestic service only after becoming seriously ill through constant attendance of her sick mother. The doctor informed Mrs Legh of her condition and she sent her coach to bring Hester to Adlington for recuperation.

In the meantime, the evangelical influence of David Simpson on St Michael's had brought it to a point of crisis through a mixture of doctrinal controversy and petty jealousy. The first signs of trouble came when Thomas Hewson, the first curate, insisted on preaching as often as he liked, to the exclusion of Simpson. Many in the congregation objected to the barring of the dynamic young curate from the pulpit and expressed anger in part by anonymous newspaper letters. A 'peace meeting' temporarily brought about an agreement under which the balance of preaching appointments between the two men was restored. The truce was broken before the end of 1773 when Hewson refused to allow Simpson to take part in either of the two services on 26 December. When he repeated the restriction on the afternoon of the following Sunday, many of the congregation followed Hewson home to express their anger. A hastily convened parochial meeting again restored peace, but it was not to last. Matters came to a head when Simpson felt he could no longer tolerate Hewson's dull preaching and decided to expose him to the point of humiliation. He chose to time his attack on the day when both men were asked to preach 'charity sermons', Hewson in the morning and Simpson in the afternoon. When Simpson started to preach, it immediately became clear that his text was the same one that Hewson had used in the morning. When he realised what Simpson was doing, he leapt from his seat, rushed up to the pulpit and threw Simpson to the ground. The church was soon in uproar with members of the congregation taking sides. In the middle of the mayhem,

Charles Roe shouted that as a friend of Simpson's if the pulpit was closed to him, he would build a church for him.[96]

This incident prompted Hewson to bar Simpson completely and to submit a formal complaint about him to the Bishop of Chester. The Bishop might have been more favourably disposed to David Simpson had it not been for objections to his preaching from another influential quarter. It had come to Simpson's knowledge that young women leaving the security of their families to enter service in the houses of the wealthy were in acute moral danger. In particular he became aware that one of the local squires made no secret of the fact that he was in the habit of regularly seducing his maids. Now there was little point in preaching Sunday by Sunday about the perils of sin if one ignored the disgraceful behaviour of that kind on the part of someone who was supposed to be setting an example, even if he happened to be a personal friend of the Bishop and sitting in the family pew facing one. David Simpson did not mince his words.

> Some pride themselves much upon their birth, rank and family and look down with contempt upon those they regard as ignoble and vulgar and contend there is no great harm in corrupting and debauching the daughter of a poor person, whose family and connections make no great figure in the world. If it were a young lady of family and fortune that were to be seduced, the affair would then be of a very serious nature. But give me leave to ask – is not a poor person's daughter equally valuable in the eyes of an indulgent, though poor parent, and equally precious in the impartial eyes of heaven? Ah Sirs! Such boasted superiority of birth, family, riches, honours, reason, learning and understanding is cheap, very cheap, in the eyes of God. Better indeed is the humble cottage swain, who lives in innocence, obscurity and sweet simplicity, and who loves, obeys and worships his God, than all the sons and daughters of pleasure, family and reputation, who, by their private or public vices render themselves the scourge of mankind and the pests of all virtuous society.[97]

A second protest to the Bishop, a closing of the ranks of the establishment and David Simpson was temporarily suspended from preaching in the church of which he was second curate. His biographer in the *Methodist Magazine* of 1813 expressed his own views on the causes and consequences of this action:

His enemies were the enemies of the gospel ... Had his preaching accorded with their corrupt views of religion, had his preaching and practice proved congenial with their worldly character, a man of such talents, so amiable a man in temper and manners, must have been hailed by them as their favourite preacher and excellent friend. But despising and rejecting that way of salvation, which so illustriously displays the sovereignty and holiness of God, how could they receive and honour him, whose every sermon bore testimony against the pride of Pharisaism and the licentiousness of the ungenerate heart? His adversaries were active, determined, united and, as they thought, successful ... In future years it will be considered as a most extraordinary circumstance in the annals of British ecclesiastical history, that so many of the clergy should have encountered the bitterest opposition for no other 'crime' than that of preaching the doctrines of those very articles, without subscribing to which they could not have been admitted to Episcopal ordination! This was the only crime for which Mr Simpson had been persecuted from two curacies, and in the last instance, by the imperious mandate of metropolitan authority.

How long he remained under suspicion we are not informed. However, we know that he was not idle, that such was his zeal for the glory of God, and compassion for the souls of men, that he could find no rest but in his wonted ministerial labours. During that period, he made frequent excursions into the unenlightened parts of the neighbouring country, preaching in private houses, and wherever he saw the door of usefulness thrown open. This practice he continued occasionally afterwards as long as he was able, and it was attended with such evident affects, in the conversion of sinners from the error of their ways, that, to the end of his ministry, he considered these itinerant labours as the most successful of his whole life. When remarking upon this subject to a friend, that his health would no longer permit him to follow the same plan, 'The Methodist preachers', he said, 'are now generally received and societies are formed in those villages; so that I do not see the same necessity as before'.[98]

The controversy at St Michael's was never settled, but David Simpson was Charles Roe's man and the pride of the leading citizen in the town simply could not allow him to accept the virtual dismissal of his protégé. His declaration in St Michael's followed an earlier vow that that if he was successful in business he would build a church as an expression of gratitude to God for his prosperity. The suspension of David Simpson convinced him that the time to act on those vows had come. He bought a piece of land no more than 200 yards from St Michael's and Christ Church, with David Simpson installed as its first incumbent, was opened on Christmas Day 1775.

The building of Christ Church was an early manifestation of the rising power of the middle class usurping the authority of the old order. Christ Church was legally established within the Church of England through the passing of a special Act of Parliament, but it was a church without a parish and its incumbent's official appointment remained that of a second curate at St Michael's. Because the church was not put under Episcopal jurisdiction, the Bishop of Chester refused to consecrate it. He simply ignored it and acted as though it did not exist.

According to the Rev. John Gaulter, Simpson's biographer in 1799, it was during his period of banishment from the pulpit that the prime curacy at St Michael's became vacant and that in his capacity as mayor, the office in which the nomination resided, Mr Rowland Gould offered the position to David Simpson, who accepted it.[99] This was not the case. When Charles Roe decided to erect his own church the mayor was John Ryle, the Methodist, and the prime curacy was held by Thomas Hewson until his death in 1778 when Gould was mayor.[100]

What becomes clear from this corrected chronology is that in 1778, when Christ Church had already been operating for almost three years, a bold attempt was made to install David Simpson as prime curate back at St Michael's. Had this been successful, it would have given Charles Roe effective control over both Anglican churches in the town. This audacious move was entirely typical of Charles Roe and illustrates that in ecclesiastical affairs, as in matters of business, he was both decisive and ruthless.

No wonder the officers at St Michael's were incensed. They were faced with the imminent prospect of the young curate, with his unacceptable Methodist inclinations and his record of having taken most of their congregation to a new church round the corner, either reoccupying their pulpit or appointing an assistant with similar views, responsible to him. A fresh petition against David Simpson was submitted to the Bishop and 17 grounds of objection were listed. All these were dismissed except one – that he was a Methodist or that his preaching greatly tended to increase the number of Methodists.

To that single charge he pleaded guilty by letter:

This is true. My method is to preach the great truths and doctrines and precepts of the gospel in as plain and earnest and affectionate a manner as I am able. Persons of different ranks, persuasions and characters come to hear. Some hereby have been convinced of the error of their ways, they see their guilt and the danger they are in and become seriously concerned about their salvation. The change is soon discovered; they meet with one or another who invites them to attend the preachings and meetings among the Methodists, and hence their number is increased to a considerable degree. This is the truth. I own the fact, I have often thought of it, but I confess myself unequal to the difficulty. What would your lordship advise?

The Bishop of Chester accepted the petition and refused to endorse the nomination. Perhaps as consolation, Charles Roe promoted him to be Vicar of Christ Church in the following year, 1779.

Chapter 11

Hester's ordeal in nursing her sick mother at a time of her own illness and her period of recuperation lasted many months. The episode became part of Methodist folklore and as late as 1909 Joseph Ritson, in relating the story of a pioneering Primitive Methodist travelling preacher, recalled that 'in her girlhood, she associated herself with the chapel and like Hester Ann Rogers, was subjected to severe persecution on this account by her mother, who frequently compelled her to go without breakfast and dinner on the Sabbath'.[101]

There are a number of reasons why Hester's account of her conversion experience was so attractive to later generations. In the first place it was an exposure of the 'interior landscape of the experience of the heart'.[102], expressed with clarity and conviction which could be used as a standard for those seeking a similar spiritual awakening. Secondly, it was specifically prompted by the reading of the Wesley sermon on the doctrine that was at the core of Methodist theology. Thirdly, it was the conversion of someone with a background similar to that of Wesley himself; the daughter of a clergyman, strictly brought up, with a strong desire to lead a good life and yet lacking an assurance of salvation. Lastly, she had quite deliberately rejected all the trappings of life in high society at considerable personal cost, in order to maintain a total loyalty to the Methodist society. It should be added, at those times when the authorities were suspicious of any religious movement with revivalist tendencies, fearing that mass emotion might promote political revolution, it was convenient to have a record of a conversion which was experienced outside the emotional hothouse of a 'fervent Methodist society meeting'.[103]

Having partially recovered, Hester returned home and received a letter from her godmother. Her reply, dated 12 November 1775, demonstrates her impeccable manners, her literary skills, her firm understanding of Methodist doctrine and her absolute determination not to be diverted from her spiritual pilgrimage.

> Dear and Honoured Madam,
> I beg leave to return you my most sincere and humble thanks for your kind letter and advice, as you are so kind to express a concern on my account, I hope you will pardon the liberty, and allow me to say what is my opinion and belief, and on what alone I can build any hopes of heaven and happiness.

Hester then bases her theological stance on the Fall, the 'guilt of Adam and the depravity of soul which he contracted'. God's answer is the provision of 'an all-sufficient ransom, even his well-beloved Son!' She then sets out three essentials for salvation:

> First, a perfect obedience to the divine law; secondly, an infinitely meritorious satisfaction to the law and government of God, for the dishonour brought upon them by the sin of man; thirdly, a restoration of the moral image of God to the soul, which image was lost by the fall of man. The first of these was completed by the life of our Redeemer, the second by his death; and the third is affected by the Holy Ghost.

She proceeds with a well-presented argument, based on biblical texts, that justification comes through 'faith without the deeds of the law'. In case the content of the latter lacks clarity or her doctrine as explained is regarded as heretical, she politely requests; 'If you will be kind enough to read the eleventh, twelfth and thirteenth Articles of the Church of England, they will farther explain my meaning.'

Having demonstrated the orthodoxy of her faith, Hester feels free to explain her conviction of the necessity of spiritual renewal, which takes her beyond David Simpson's sermons to the heart of John Wesley's emphases:

There is a third thing also necessary to our salvation; which is, that the image of God be restored to the soul. Now this is done in regeneration. Our Saviour assures us 'except a man be born again, he cannot see the kingdom of God'. And again, 'except ye be converted and become as little children ye shall not enter into the kingdom of heaven'. Nor are we fit for it till renewed by the Spirit of God. For, were it possible to be admitted there, we could not enjoy the pure and spiritual delights of the saints above. Their joy consists in an entire freedom from all sin and corruption; and in serving, adoring and praising the Father of all their mercies, the Son of his love, and the Spirit of holiness. And they are so far from being weary of this, that they think eternity too short to utter all his praise! How irksome would be an eternity spent in this manner, to a person who never had his affections spiritualised, and his will brought into conformity to the will of God! There is a change which must be wrought in this world; for there is no repentance in the grave; as death leaves us, judgment will find us. Then, 'he that is unjust shall be unjust still; he that is filthy shall be filthy still; he that is righteous shall be righteous still; and he that is holy shall be holy still!' The Holy Ghost is author of this conversion of new birth; for no man hath quickened his own soul. It is He that must begin, carry on, and complete it. 'Now, if any man have not the Spirit of Christ, he is none of his.' And the fruits of this Spirit is 'love, joy, peace, long-suffering, gentleness, goodness, faith, meekness, temperance: against such there is no law. And they that are Christ's have crucified the flesh with its affections and lusts. If any man be in Christ he is a new creature; old things are passed away; behold all things are become new'. And Jesus Christ is made of God unto us wisdom, righteousness, sanctification and redemption; that, according as it is written, He that glorifieth, let him glory in God. God forbid that I should glory, save in the cross of our Lord Jesus Christ, by whom the world is crucified unto me, and I unto the world.'

The last paragraph of the letter reveals how much strain Hester's conduct had put on family friendships and the distress it caused her mother.

> This, dear Madam, is what I believe; and this, I think, is agreeable to the word of God, and to the Articles and Homilies of the Church of England; and no schism of the church of Christ. Forfeiting your love and friendship is a great trial; but, believe me, when I think of seeking salvation in any other way, it seems as a sword piercing my very heart! And seeing my dear mother so very unhappy on my account, gives me more grief than I can express: and the thought of being so detrimental to her in worldly things, and that my conduct should make you less her friend, seems strange, and to me is very afflicting; but I think these things ought not to be urged too far, especially where the soul is concerned.
>
> I am afraid I have tried your patience; so will hasten to subscribe myself, honoured Madam, Your obliged and dutiful god-daughter,
>
> H.A. Roe

Mrs Roe was not the only senior member of the family to have trouble with an offspring. On 17 October 1775, Robert Roe was converted and he, along with five of his brothers and sisters, joined the Methodist society against the wishes of their father, Charles.

So the man who had married a Methodist but forbidden her from associating with the movement locally, but had supported his niece when she was threatened with eviction, suddenly found himself with six rebellious children. No wonder he pointed an accusing finger at Hester when calling his son Robert to account: 'He said my cousin had been the ruin of all his children.'[104]

Chapter 12

Even with the benefit of hindsight, it is difficult to understand why Methodism should have brought so much controversy to the Roe family. The reason Charles Roe refused his second wife the local association with the Methodists she longed for had nothing to do with doctrine and by supporting David Simpson in the dispute of 1774, he provided a pulpit for a man who was openly sympathetic to the Methodist cause. Not only that, but when Simpson subsequently accepted a charge of actively helping Methodism to expand in rural areas, Roe responded by promoting him. Co-operating with the Methodists went farther than this.

> For a period of over 20 years until his death in 1799, Simpson welcomed the Methodists to his church each Sunday morning and took his own congregation, excluding the senior members of the Roe family, to the Methodist chapel in the afternoon. ... Furthermore he counselled the local preachers and even attended the Methodist Conference in 1784.[105]

According to Rosa E. Gladding, Simpson 'made more Methodists in Macclesfield than even Wesley himself; the whole town's life in its multifarious interests was lifted by his strenuous labours on to a higher plane. An elegy written at his death by one of the Methodist preachers begins:

> 'Tis done! 'tis done! 'Tis now for ever o'er,
> Simpson the man of God is now no more.[106]

When Brunswick Chapel, Macclesfield, was opened in 1824 by the Rev. Jabez Bunting, who had married the daughter of Simpson's organist, there were services in the morning, afternoon and evening, each having a congregation of 1,500 people.

By the unanimous request of the trustees, the Morning Service of the Established Church was read in the forenoon. The opening of the Second Chapel in Macclesfield was considered a fit opportunity to accommodate the views of several persons who first became partakers of salvation under the Ministry of the late David Simpson and whose attachment to Methodism was considered as consequently associated with a just veneration for the sound, ancient and impressive Liturgy of the Church of England.[107]

In 1998, the Silk History Group, a sub-group of the Friends of Macclesfield Silk Heritage, published the results of its research of the work and influence of David Simpson. 'He was an amateur physician, a legal adviser to the poor and the founder of Macclesfield's educational system. Beginning by teaching the poor children of the town in his home, he persuaded his friends to do the same.'[108] It was through his lasting influence that Macclesfield Sunday school was erected in Roe Street.[109] Bearing in mind Simpson's impeccable Methodist credentials, it might well be wondered why Hester and her cousins should have bothered with the Methodists when they could so easily have saved themselves a lot of trouble by staying under the ministrations of the man who was preaching the same evangelical doctrines from the pulpit of what was, in effect, their own family church.

The reason can be found in Hester's journal. It was in the fellowship of the Methodist society that she came to understand fully the nature of the Methodist spiritual journey from awareness of sin, to repentance, to faith, to assurance and, finally, to holiness. Hester's journal, the published evidence of those closest to her and her surviving letters, all confirm that from the time of her conversion she had a deep assurance of faith which never waned. Typical of her diary entries is one for 12 February 1777; 'To know God is mine, to feel he dwelleth in my heart, ruleth my will, my affections, my tempers, my desires, to know he loveth me ten thousand times better that I love him: O, it is unspeakable salvation.'[110]

David Simpson was an Anglican Methodist, John Wesley had a foot in both camps, but Hester, like many of her contemporaries who had no background in the Established Church, was primarily a Methodist. The difference lay in the nature of spiritual experience, Hester's great gift, and Andrew Worth points to the significance of her meeting with David Simpson, when she gave him her personal testimony and he readily acknowledged that she possessed a quality that he envied;

> Mr Simpson asked me many questions respecting my experience, and I freely told him what the Lord had done and is doing for me. He said, 'I wish I felt the same. I long for it, and I believe it is the privilege of the children of God, though too few enjoy it. Let no one discourage you, Miss Roe, for what you experience is of God. You need never lose it and I hope you will pray that I may attain it.' My soul truly rejoiced to hear him speak thus. Lord baptise thy servant with thy Spirit.[111]

Gail Malmgreen refers to David Simpson's 'unresolved dilemma of choice between his position as an Anglican clergyman and the fuller, warmer, freer, spiritual atmosphere offered by the Methodists'.[112]

This was more a matter of style than substance, but the difference was of significance to Hester. 'Mr H. preached at the new church ... But though he preaches the real Gospel, yet I cannot find the same unction attending his words as does that of God's servants among the Methodists.'[113]

Hester's spiritual maturity had developed within a Methodist movement that had as its objective the spreading of 'scriptural holiness through the land'. Paul Smith reminds us that in case it might be suspected that this term, first used at the 1744 Conference, was an incidental remark, perhaps taken out of context, it should be pointed out that it was repeated at every Conference for the succeeding 26 years.[114]

Knowledge of the way in which this theory of spirituality manifested itself in individual lives is essential to any understanding of the early Methodists. Their central and dominant emotion was love, responding to a love they deemed to come from God. Joy was a characteristic of their emotional state. It will be recalled that in the immediate aftermath of John Wesley's experience of the 'warmed heart' on 24 May 1738, he faced a problem:

> But it was not long before the enemy suggested 'This cannot be faith, for where is thy joy?' Then I was taught that peace and victory over sin are essential to faith in the Captain of our salvation; but that, as to the transports of joy that usually attend the beginning of it, especially in those who have mourned deeply, God sometimes giveth, sometimes with-holdeth them, according to the counsels of His own will. [115]

Hester did not suffer from any similar post-conversion depression and by the time John Wesley visited Macclesfield in the spring of 1776 her physical condition was in a fragile state, but spiritually she was more mature that John Wesley had been in May 1738.

Chapter 13

On Monday 1 April 1776, John Wesley visited Macclesfield and on the following day preached on Parsonage Green, not far from the house of Alderman Ryle; 'There are no mockers here and scarce an inattentive hearer. So mightily has the word of God prevailed.'[116]

On the Wednesday morning, Hester met him for the first time when they had an hour together just after breakfast before he travelled to Manchester. Such was her appearance that he gave her his opinion that she was suffering from tuberculosis and did not hesitate to repeat his instant diagnosis in his first letter to her. It might well be thought that this is an unsuitable communication to be sent to a 20-year-old young lady who is not in the best of health.

3 May 1776, Whitehaven
With pleasure I sit down to write to my dear Miss Roe, who has been much upon my mind since I left Macclesfield ... I am afraid I shall hardly see you again till we meet in the Garden of God. But if you should gradually decay, if you be sensible of the hour approaching, when your spirit is to return to God: I should be glad to have notice of it, wherever I am, that if possible I might see you once more before you

> Clap your glad wing and soar away,
> And mingle with the blaze of day.

Perhaps in such a circumstance, I might be of some little comfort to your dear mama, who would stand in much need of comfort; and it may be, our blessed Master would enable me to teach you at once, and learn of you, to die! How far does the corruptible and decaying body press down the soul? Your disorder naturally sinks the spirit, and occasions heaviness and dejection. Can you, notwithstanding this, rejoice evermore, and in everything, give thanks?

> My dear Hetty,
> Yours affectionately
> J Wesley[117]

Hester might well have taken offence, but she did not regard illness and the prospect of death as matters of concern.

> He behaved to me with parental tenderness, and greatly rejoiced in the Lord's goodness to his soul: encouraged me to hold fast, and to declare what the Lord had wrought. He thinks me consumptive, but welcome life, or welcome death, for Christ is mine.[118]

John Wesley ends his letter with a request to Hester to enter a continuing correspondence with him in the limited time she has left: 'If it will not hurt you, I desire you will write often ...'

It is not likely that he spent more than a passing moment composing a few words of 'consolation' to a 'dying' girl in the middle of a hectic schedule in the north-east of England at the beginning of May 1776. However, John Wesley was wrong in his diagnosis and as Hester survived and enthusiastically responded to his invitation to 'write often', the relationship developed. Most of Wesley's personal papers were destroyed shortly after his death, including the letters Hester sent to him. Fortunately she copied and retained several of those she had written and it is plain from these and from those he sent to her, that these two people, separated in age by over 50 years, were kindred spirits. She sought advice from him and he readily gave it once he had got used to the idea that her illness was not terminal. His second letter, from Newcastle-on-Tyne on 2 June 1776 is virtually an obituary. 'I could almost say it is hard that I should see you once and no more. But it is a comfort, that to die is not to be lost. Our union will be more full and perfect hereafter.

Surely our disembodied souls shall join,
Surely my friendly shade shall mix with thine.[119]

Hester wrote to him on 28 August 1776 and it is clear from his reply on 16 September that she had explained all the problems facing her cousins in the tension of their relationship with their father because of their association with the Methodists. His advice is general and scripturally based: 'I hope though your cousins are tried they will not be discouraged; then all these things will "work together for good". Probably if they stand firm, religion will, in a while, leaven the whole family. But they will have need of much patience, as well as much resolution.'[120] Then he displays humour in expressing satisfaction that blame for this family strife has been directed at her: 'I am not sorry that you have met with a little blame in the affair, and I hope it was not undeserved. Happy are they that suffer for well-doing! I was almost afraid that all men would speak well of you.'[121]

That letter of 16 September 1776 is written in terms of intimate affection.

... I was beginning to grow a little apprehensible lest your love was declining; but you have sweetly dispelled all my apprehensions of that sort ... Do you feel no intermission of your happiness in God? Do you never find any lowness of spirits? Does time never hang heavy upon your hands? How is your health? You see how inquisitive I am, because everything relating to you concerns me. I once thought I could not be well acquainted with any one till many years had elapsed; and yet I am as well acquainted with you as if I had known you from infancy. You are now my comfort and joy![122]

In his book relating the story of Ann Bolton, John Banks refers to the trouble caused within the Wesley's marriage by John's expressions of affection in his correspondence with his female friends.

The question is ... had she (his wife) any cause to be jealous? It must be said at once that Wesley's relationship with his female correspondents was completely unsexual. He wrote to his wife on 9 December 1774: 'The subject of our correspondence was heart religion, the inward Kingdom of God, you have both their letters and mine.'

This is barely understood in the 20th and 21st centuries, especially when the language in which he wrote to them sometimes included what we could consider sexual overtones ... It is also true that Wesley wrote in terms of affection to men as well as women. Moreover Wesley wrote with great openness and warmth. Perhaps he considered himself beyond the reach of personal danger, and perhaps he was right.[123]

H.D. Rack comments that 'Wesley was often at his best in these relationships'.[124] This cannot be said of the younger Wesley, quite unable to come to terms with his emotions due to 'some deep-rooted psychological disability in his nature as regards relationships with women'.[125] Perhaps when they no longer posed either a threat or an emotional challenge, he could relax, even if his letters were capable of being misunderstood.

In literally thousands of entries in her journal and in her letters to her friends, Hester always refers to 'Dear Mr Wesley'. The tone of her language is affectionate but temperate. Several years later, Hester's relationship with a member of the opposite sex would come under severe 18th-century criticism and test 21st-century attitudes. On that occasion, the man in question was not John Wesley.

Chapter 14

In reading the letters John Wesley wrote to Hester Roe in the years immediately after their first meeting, it is possible to gain a clear understanding of those two distinct aspects of Methodist doctrine, assurance and holiness, and the relationship between them.

Liverpool, 10 April 1781
My Dear Hetty,
... The periphery (or full measure of faith) is such a clear conviction of being now in the favour of God, as excludes all doubt and fear concerning it. The full measure of hope, is such a clear confidence in the person who possesses it, that he shall enjoy the glory of God, as excludes all doubt and fear concerning this. And this confidence is totally different from an opinion that 'no saint shall fall from grace'. It has, indeed, no relation to it. Bold presumptious men often substitute this base counterfeit, in the room of that precious confidence. But, it is observable, the opinion remains just as strong while men are sinning and serving the devil, as while they are serving God. Holiness or unholiness does not affect it in the least degree. Whereas the giving way to any thing unholy, either in heart or life, immediately clouds the full assurance of hope, which cannot subsist any longer than the heart cleaves steadfastly to God.[126]

London, 7 January 1782
My Dear Hetty,
In the success of Mr Leech's preaching, we have one proof of a thousand, that the blessing of God always attends the publishing of full salvation as attainable now by simple faith. You should always have in readiness that little Tract, 'The Plain Account of

Christian Perfection'; there is nothing that would so effectually stop the mouths of those, who call this a 'new doctrine'. All who thus object, are really (though they suspect nothing less) seeking sanctification by works. If it be by works, then certainly these will need time, in order to the doing of these works. But if it is by faith, it is plain, a moment is as a thousand years. Then God says, (in the spiritual as in the outward world) 'Let there be light', and there is light ...[127]

John Wesley was not only impressed by Hester's piety, he was also appreciative of her ability to explain the depth of her spiritual experience in her letters. On 6 October 1776 he wrote, '... I cannot express the satisfaction I receive from your open and artless manner of writing, especially when you speak of the union of spirit which you feel with'.[128]

Hester is not content to regard the letters from John Wesley only as personal devotional aids, she uses them in her own letters to press her friends to search for faith and, beyond that, to holiness. In writing to Mr Francis Swindells of Leek on 20 October 1780, she emphasises the necessity of faith in obtaining salvation.

Then in a letter to her cousin Robert Roe of 23 November 1776, she urges him to seek sanctification beyond that first step of faith.

'... The privileges of the justified soul are very great ... never rest till all your evil nature be destroyed and every root of bitterness plucked up, till you have given God all your loving heart.' Next comes her own testimony of assurance: 'O what a present heaven of love I feel.'[129]

When Robert questions the validity of Hester's experience of a sense of holiness that emanates directly from acceptance of this aspect of faith, she hastens to enlighten him. '... You ask me if I am not in a delusion respecting my experience of perfect love. Blessed be God I have not a shadow of a doubt, even Satan himself finds these suggestions vain.'[130]

Throughout the period in which this correspondence is being conducted between the two cousins, Robert is at Oxford University reading for his degree in Theology. His letters were never published, but it is possible to glean from her replies that he is testing her statements either with his professors or among his fellow students. In the 1770s, theological conclusions based even partially on emotion and experience would be dismissed out of hand. Bearing in mind that she has been given no formal theological training and her academic studies have been limited to private reading and receiving words of wisdom from John Wesley, either directly or through her presence in the Methodist society, her manner of dealing with Robert's questions is remarkable. She displays a mature grasp of the arguments he puts to her and has no difficulty in establishing a clear advantage in the intellectual debate. This is ironic because she regards the Oxford method of subjecting faith to mere reasoning as irrelevant. The gospel is to be believed, not argued about – argument is a waste of time and energy and diverts attention from the things that matter.

In her letter of 29 April 1779, she advises Robert to follow God 'blindfold' and on the 12 August protests that she would have avoided 'distinctions', but for her sense of duty in answering his questions. His particular concern is the relationship of faith to works. She stresses that 'works is not a meritorious condition, but the use of the grace given to us'. God loves all mankind unconditionally. 'We are required to use the light given ... the forsaking of sin is an act of man and a condition we are commanded to act faith.'[131]

On 14 January Hester takes issue with him. His studies are coming to an end and he has the prospect of being offered a curacy; surely the time for arguing has passed. He is supposed to be a leader of the flock.[132]

Hester's letters to Miss Loxdale repeat the advice to keep clear of 'opinions'. She prefers to keep to Scripture and on 30 June of the previous year had advised her friend to put 'prayer before disputations'. Miss Loxdale evidently has acquaintances who are questioning the doctrine of Christian Perfection and Hester urges her to 'avoid the company of those who love vain controversy'.[133] Her advice on the same topic on 4 August 1779 is specific.

Mr Fletcher's Polemical Essay, especially his Address to imperfect believers seeking Christian Perfection, was made a great blessing to me. This, with Mr Wesley's

Plain Account answered every objection, every doubt, and I earnestly recommend them to your serious perusal.[134]

If there was one person who could teach Hester more about the doctrine of Christian Perfection than John Wesley, it was John Fletcher of Madeley. Andrew Worth refers to her journal entry relating several interviews she had with him in 1781 when he fully explained to her the doctrine of the purity of the heart:

He (Fletcher) lifted up his eyes and heart to heaven, and exclaimed: 'Bless her Heavenly Father!' It seemed as if an instant answer was given and a beam of glory let down! I was filled with deep humility and love, yea my whole soul overflowed with unutterable sweetness.[135]

By this time Hester, still only 25 years of age, was a very mature Christian indeed. Almost every word she wrote could well have been written under the direct guidance of John Wesley, but there is a crucial difference between them; Wesley's role was that of pastor – Hester wrote from personal experience.

CHAPTER 15

By 1780 the success of Charles Roe in his business affairs was matched by his failure to control his growing family. His sons gave him the greatest trouble, especially Robert who had repeatedly been refused ordination by bishops and college authorities because of his unwillingness to withdraw from the Methodists. Charles did his best to secure his son's ordination, but his influence outside his home-town was insignificant. Had Robert been willing to compromise, the matter would have been settled quickly, but he was not to be persuaded and was forbidden to enter his father's house or even visit the town.[136]

Joseph continued to be connected with the Methodists, but had established his independence elsewhere and, consequently, had no communication with his father.

Charles Roe junior had succumbed to his father's pressure to abandon Methodism, but any comfort Charles senior might have gained from this measure of obedience was more than lost by his son's subsequent wild behaviour and eventual marriage against his father's will.

Neither William nor Samuel were prepared to tread that narrow path of conformity which would have denied them a life of extravagance on one side and the spiritual delights of Methodism on the other.

Only the daughters seemed to manage to combine conformity to paternal discipline and a continuing association with Methodism through attendance at the Methodist chapel with David Simpson and friendship with their cousin Hester Ann. For reasons that had prompted him to intervene on behalf of Hester several years earlier, Charles had no wish to evict his daughters and it was impracticable for this busy entrepreneur to control all their activities once they reached the age of maturity. On the other hand, defiance on the part of a son was a serious matter that called for decisive action.

In these circumstances, it seems remarkable that David Simpson had the freedom to maintain his close association with the Methodists to the point of being allowed to invite John Wesley to occupy his pulpit, a privilege denied to Wesley in every other Anglican church in Cheshire at that time. Yet Simpson, who had readily acknowledged his support of Methodism when charged with the 'offence' by the Bishop of Chester, was quite prepared to do his utmost to persuade Robert to leave Methodism in accordance with the wishes of his father. This must have stretched the obligations of patronage to their limits.

While Robert was with friends in Bristol in the autumn of 1780, he met John Wesley and went with him to visit a Mr Castleman. By his own testimony Robert was in a poor state of health, so much so that the host did not consider him to be in any condition to travel. 'At night,' he said, 'it is a shame this poor, weak thing should go home tonight; let him have my bed; but I declined it.'[137]

Robert was not the only member of the family whose health was in decline. News reached him in October that his brother, Samuel, was dying and that his father was dangerously ill. Hoping for reconciliation, he travelled north to Chesterfield where his father was staying. Charles reluctantly agreed to see him for an hour and, typically, offered him the prospect of acceptance if he would agree to marry an eligible young lady who happened to possess a personal fortune of over £10,000. Not surprisingly, Robert declined the offer. In normal circumstances that would have ended the meeting without further ceremony, but Charles was concerned that every attempt should be made to save the life of his son, Samuel, and he agreed that Robert should travel with the family back to Macclesfield on condition that he should then accompany Samuel to Bristol where he could receive the best medical help available at that time. Robert readily agreed, travelled south with his brother, and Charles and his wife joined them in Bath a short while afterwards.

Samuel's condition deteriorated still further and, recognising that he had not long to live, asked that he be taken home where he could say farewell to his friends and receive the ministrations of David Simpson. Again Robert accompanied his brother, who was laid on a bed in a long carriage drawn by six horses. Samuel survived the journey only as far as Leek, just 13 miles short of his intended destination and a few days later his body was laid to rest in the new family vault in Christ Church.

Charles Roe and his wife remained in Bath so that after the funeral, Robert was left in residence in the family home. Although Charles Roe made known his displeasure at Robert's presence in the house from which he had been banished, he gave no instruction that he should be removed and this left him undisturbed for a period of over three months.

If it might be said that Methodism haunted Charles Roe in his lifetime, it might also be concluded that, had it been within his power, he would have haunted Methodism after his death. Throwing caution to the winds, Robert invited two Methodist preachers, Samuel Bardsley and James Rogers, to join him there and organised prayer meetings.

Just two days before John Wesley's annual visit to the town on Thursday 29 March 1781, Robert Roe invited his cousin, Hester Ann, to meet his friends and it was at the house of her uncle that she saw James Rogers for the first time.

Shortly afterwards, Charles Roe and his wife returned from Bath. Robert's continued presence was tolerated by his ailing father, but his Methodist activities were temporarily suspended.

Charles Roe was not to live much longer. The fact that his reconciliation with Robert was less than complete is revealed in Robert's personal note, written in April 1781: 'My father is worse, sometimes my heart seems ready to break with grief, at others, it feels as hard as stone. Lord save his soul, for Christ's sake.'[138]

Nothing is more likely to bring disunity to a large family more than the prospect of inheritance immediately prior to the death of a wealthy man. Both Robert and Joseph had been banished so were not likely to be named as beneficiaries in the will. But Robert was present and the question arose as to whether or not Joseph ought to be informed of his father's imminent passing. These considerations bring out the worst in people, but, despite some opposition, Joseph was summoned. He rode non-stop for 200 miles, but failed to reach his father in time. All the others had been called, one by one, to be blessed and forgiven for any behaviour that had caused distress to their father.

On 30 April 1781, Robert called on Hester.

> Cousin Robert came all in tears; and says that his father is altered much for the worse, that he sees his danger, and calls frequently for Mr Simpson to pray with him. This morning he gave orders concerning his temporal concerns, and then took leave of my aunt and all his children.'[139]

Charles Roe died on Thursday 3 May and Hester describes his elaborate funeral on 8 May:

> In the dusk of the evening my uncle's remains were carried in great pomp, by his own carriage and horses, to the New Church, and accompanied by coaches, torches, and a vast concourse of people; but the horses unaccustomed to be adorned with such trappings as black cloth, escutcheons etc, would hardly proceed. He was interred by Mr Simpson in the vault he had so lately prepared! Yes, this much feared and much loved man is now committed to corruption and worms![140]

The family's speculation about the destiny of the fortune of Charles Roe was thrown into confusion when it was discovered that he had not left a will. Benjamin Smith aptly describes the consequence as a 'distressing estrangement'[141] of the Roe children and eventually the estate was divided according to the advice of 'Aunt Stockdale', the sister of the mother of most of them, but who was trusted by all. There is a considerable irony in the fact that the estate of that pioneer industrialist and implacable opponent of Methodism was administered by a long-standing friend of John Wesley.

Chapter 16

Most of John Wesley's visits to Macclesfield lasted no more than a few hours, but in the spring of 1782, he arranged a longer stay that extended over the Easter weekend. Following the death of Charles Roe, there was not the slightest restriction to his preaching for his friend, David Simpson at Christ Church. Hester met him on Thursday 28 March.

I went to meet my dear friend Miss Salmon at Mrs Clulow's house where I also found John Sellars and Mrs Clulow from Chester. Mr Wesley arrived soon after and I drank tea with him at Mr Ryle's. I think he is more alive and full of God than ever.[142]

If it were not for Hester's diary, the only record of that weekend would be in John Wesley's published journal which covers the three days from Good Friday to Easter Sunday in a single page and the only detail given concerns the Christ Church organ.

Friday 29 March (being Good Friday)
I came to Macclesfield just time enough to assist Mr Simpson in the laborious service of the day. I preached for him morning and afternoon; and we administered sacrament to about 1,300 persons. While we were administering I heard a low, soft solemn sound, just like that of an Aeolian harp. It continued five or six minutes, and so affected many that they could not refrain from tears. It then gradually died away. Strange that no other organist (that I know) should think of this. In the evening I preached at our room. Here was that harmony which art cannot imitate.[143]

A footnote in the published journal records that after the service Wesley complimented the organist: 'Mr MacLardie, if I could ensure a similar performance to yours this afternoon I would have an organ introduced into every one of our chapels.'[144]

Hester adds a few details:

> Good Friday – He preached in the New Church in the morning from 'Ye know the grace of our Lord Jesus Christ' and in the afternoon from 'Wherefore laying aside all malice and guile'. At night in our own Chapel from 'I beseech you as strangers and pilgrims'. I spent some time with him alone over the weekend and he behaved with fatherly affection. I had never more solid comfort in his company, never found it more truly profitable.[145]

John Wesley's journal entry for Saturday 30 March is brief:

> As our friends at Leek, 13 miles from Macclesfield, would take no denial, I went over and preached about noon to a lovely congregation. God bore witness to His word in an uncommon manner, so that I could not think much of my labour.[146]

John Wesley's journal contains literally thousands of entries of a similar kind as he travelled and preached for over half a century. But this short visit to Leek in 1782, was far from typical for two reasons. First, the event was reported in detail by an eye-witness who had been trained in early childhood to recall the content of her father's sermons and, second, so far as Methodism was concerned, Leek was alien territory. According to the Rev. J.B. Dyson:

> notwithstanding all the efforts that were made, the soil in Leek was barren and unproductive; to use the words subsequently employed by Mr Wesley, it was like 'ploughing the sand'. This was so much the case, that together with the spirit of persecution, which still ran high, the preachers became discouraged and resolved to turn their attention to some more promising portion of the Lord's vineyard, and thus to abandon Leek entirely.[147]

Dyson relates that in the mid-1770s, the Society:

> took possession of its first regular preaching-place,
> which was a Club-room down the Black Head's Yard.
> The little band being still pursued by the relentless
> spirit of persecution, were glad to adopt some plan to
> avoid their foes, and gain a little respite, and hence held
> their meetings on the week-day at 11 o'clock in the
> forenoon. [148]

In the middle of a weekend in which John Wesley,
approaching 80 years of age, preaches nine sermons in
church and chapel in Macclesfield, he is faced with the
challenge of presenting the gospel to a congregation which
comprises a handful of devoted society members swollen by a
crowd of hostile onlookers with a reputation for unruly
behaviour, attracted from the nearby market square on a
busy Saturday afternoon.

So how did John Wesley meet the challenge? An eminent
20th-century Methodist scholar repeats the image of Wesley
'preaching in the field' which was dreamed up early in the
19th century by leaders anxious to make Methodism
'respectable'.

> Emotionalism he despised as much as any modern
> sceptic ... A glance at any one of his published sermons
> – and these were the sermons, perhaps embellished by
> some illustrations, by which people were converted in
> their hundreds – will show how little Wesley valued an
> emotional appeal. [149]

Now, Wesley's sermons are masterpieces of sound
theological argument, but the notion that the scarcely
educated population of Britain was bowled over by fine
English prose, delivered in cold scholastic monotones, lacks
credibility. The written testimony of Hester Roe, after
spending most of the day with him, tells a different story.

Saturday, 30 March
Mr Wesley preached at 5 am from 'Blessed are they that
hunger and thirst after righteousness for they shall be
filled.' He addressed it chiefly to believers and offered a
free and present salvation from all sin in strong words.
One woman was set at full liberty and many were
converted and established. I breakfasted with him at
nine o'clock. He took me in his chaise to Leek, where at
one o'clock he offered salvation to all from 'The Kingdom
of heaven is at hand'. He showed first when the Gospel
of Christ is preached in any nation, city, town,
neighbourhood or family it may be said that the
Kingdom of God is set up there, or if any individual
embraces Jesus Christ and the glad tidings of salvation
by faith the kingdom of God is set up in that heart and
completed when his kingly power is manifested and all
his foes in that heart slain so that He reigns alone. Then
second, what it consists in – righteousness, peace and
joy in the Holy Ghost – and all these things begun in
Justification, but without their contraries in
Sanctification. Thus he enforced the text – This kingdom
of heaven is at hand. He addressed himself to all sorts of
people, states and conditions, old and young, yea to
children six or seven years old, drunkards, swearers,
Sabbath breakers, thieves, liars and lewd persons and
told them:

'You may now be delivered from the power of your most
besetting sins – even this day, this moment. The
kingdom of God is at hand. Serve the devil no longer, he
is a bad master, yield now to Him who loveth you, who
died for you, who will save you from all your sins here
and from hell hereafter. He loves you all, even thee thou
poor sinner. He bled for thee and wilt thou resist Him
still? Dost thou feel thou art a sinner deserving nothing
but hell? Art thou willing to know Jesus as thy Savour
and art afraid to come? Fear not, look up, He is nigh
thee. Dost thou want a pardon for all thy sins? Shall I
tell thee thou mayest have it next year, next month,
next week? Nay, I dare not. I am not sure thou canst.

Tomorrow is none of thy own. But thou mayest have it today. It is at hand. I am sent to offer it. Look up now, even this moment. Believe on the Lord Jesus Christ and thou shalt be saved. It is true that in general the work of repentance is carried on by very slow degrees. Most people are a long time after they are convinced of sin before they are Justified. But why is it? Even because of unbelief. The Word of faith is nigh thee, fear not, only believe. Art thou a child of God, a believer and feelest His kingdom in a measure set up in thy heart? Dost thou know He hath loved me and given himself for me and yet dost thou feel the remains of anger, pride, self-will, inordinate desires and affections? Then thou knowest the meaning of these words 'Tis worse than death my God to love and not my God alone'. Thou art assured 'Without holiness no man shall see the Lord', but thou art all unholy and unclean; Thou art now convinced none but God can bring a clean thing out of an unclean. Hear then His promise to thee: 'I will sprinkle water upon thee and thou shalt be clean from all filthiness and from all thy idols will I cleanse thee. A new heart will I give thee, a new spirit will I put within thee and I will take away the stony heart out of thy flesh, and I will give thee an heart of flesh, and I will put my spirit within thee and cause thee to walk in my statutes and thou shall keep my judgements and do them. I will circumcise thy heart and thou shalt love the Lord thy God with all thy heart. His will is thy Sanctification'. But art thou to wait a year, a month, a week? Art thou to stay till thou art more worthy? Not at all! Come now, a helpless sinner to a mighty Saviour. But some may say: 'Is not sanctification a gradual as well as an instantaneous work?' Yes, it is both. You may obtain a growing victory over sin from the moment you are Justified, but this is not enough. The body of sin, the carnal mind, must be destroyed and the Old Man must be slain or we cannot put on the New Man which is created after God or (which is the image of God) is righteousness and true holiness. This is done in a moment. To talk of the work being gradual would be nonsense as much as if we talked of gradual Justification. However, most persons are a long time after they are Justified before they are Sanctified wholly. But does this need to be so? Not at all! I have known a person Justified one month and Sanctified the next. Nay, I have known a person Justified in an hour and Sanctified in an hour and Glorified the next. A thousand years are with the Lord as one day, or one month or as a thousand years. 'He that believeth shall be saved.' Where art thou then, O believer who art longing for that righteousness and peace and joy in the Holy Ghost, spoken of in my text: 'The kingdom of heaven is at hand.' It is nigh thee, it is here, take it! Now believe, wait for nothing! Lord Jesus, speak to that heart, tell it: 'I am God not man.' Say unto it: 'I will, be thou clean. I am here, mighty to save – Behold me! Behold me!'

Then he prayed for penitents, for backsliders, for the unawakened, and for children, such as could till now break the Sabbath, steal apples, tell lies and disobey parents. In short, I never heard him so particular, so full of life and love and power. He wept several times while he prayed. All of the congregation were in tears and a young man who walked from Macclesfield and came to hear him in great distress of soul was set at liberty and met us praising God, who he knew had forgiven all his sins. A young boy about 10 years old wept aloud and was crying for mercy and several more appeared cut to the heart.

As we came home in the chaise Mr Wesley said: 'I never saw a more lovely congregation, Hetty, they were like melting wax, just right for divine impressions. But God was with us, there's the secret.' Tears filled his eyes.

At six o'clock he preached in our Chapel on 'God resisteth the proud and giveth grace to the humble. Humble yourselves, therefore'. His subject was wholly National Affairs, yet I found it a profitable season, but not like that at Leek.[150]

Chapter 17

It was in the Methodist 'bands' that members worked out their faith with their fellow Christians and 'It was assumed that an experience of justifying faith was shared by all those who met in bands'.[151]

D.J. Watson's research into the nature of class and band meetings in the earliest days of Methodism led him to the significant conclusion that John Wesley's motivation in establishing these meetings came from his conviction that 'only through an accountable fellowship could Christian discipleship be nurtured and made effective'.[152]

Opportunities for individuals to testify about the state of their souls were given beyond the intimacy of the band meetings in the love-feast or 'agape', a ceremony with roots in early Christianity and which Wesley had regarded 'as an extension of band fellowship and as a means of stimulating it'. They were held each quarter for men and women, separately and jointly, and were the occasion of admitting new members into the bands. When attendance was extended to all society members in 1758, it remained a highly coveted privilege, with admission strictly by class ticket only.'[153]

By 1782 Hester Roe was a member of that most exclusive of Methodist meetings, the 'select band', '... the select society, in which the doctrine of Christian perfection was most demonstrably experienced and practised'. Wesley regarded these members as 'outrunning' the greater part of their brothers and sisters, 'continually walking in the light of God and having fellowship with the Father, and with his Son Jesus Christ'.[154]

On the basis of self-accountability, Hester's credentials were impressive.

22 February 1777
One year this day, I have been wholly the Lord's and he has kept sole possession of my willing heart. Yes, thou

hast been my strength, my refuge, my guide and my merciful God; my portion, my treasure and my whole delight. One year I have loved thee with all my heart; and thou hast reigned without a rival. And now, O my Father, Saviour, Comforter, I give myself afresh to thee'.[155]

The evidence from the writings of Hester Roe about Methodist band meetings and love-feasts is not independent, far from it. She wrote from the inside as someone whose spirituality was swept along in what H.D. Rack described as 'the highly-charged atmosphere'[156] in which John Wesley operated. At intervals, psychiatrists, theologians and social and church historians have sought to apply various formulae of analysis to the dynamism of the Methodist movement, but the caution of D.L. Watson, whose book is factual rather than analytical, should be heeded: 'the Christian tradition has much to offer us if we take our forbears just as they were, and accept the integrity of their witness in its own context'.[157]

Hester gives us her own record of events in March 1782, culminating in a love-feast on the Easter Sunday evening in which the elderly John Wesley tenderly and patiently guides his flock. This testimony is unique in that it comes from personal notes Hester wrote quite separately from her journal. These have never been published and were never intended for publication. Consequently they have the highest degree of authenticity.[158]

3 March 1782
At noon in Select band I was so filled with the presence of love and Eternal Trinity that a little more and I must have dropped down at his feet. A stranger from Congleton was there who has lately received Sanctification – Mary Barker was filled with God and all present rejoiced in his precious love – especially Molly Heath who boldly declared he had cleansed her heart from all sin.

7 March 1782
I sang with grateful joy 'When all thy mercies O my God' and while I was singing that verse especially 'Thro' hidden dangers etc I had such a sense of his goodness as made my eyes o'erflow with tears.

8 March 1782
I was seized this morning with violent colic and the old pain in my side and for many hours found great difficulty in breathing, which occasioned hot and cold sweats but the thoughts that I was hastening to a blissful eternity filled me with unutterable joy. Glory be to God I have not one earthly tie – nothing but His will detains me here and I am often led to think he will use my death as a means of my mother's conversion – for he will surely hear my many prayers on her account and save her tho' it may be in the 11th hour.

12 March 1782
I met with Mr Simpson – he spoke affectionately and promised to assist the children at night in my class.

14 March 1782
At night I went with Mrs Stonehouse to G. Braddock's class. Samuel Bradshaw was leader.

15 March 1782
I called on Mrs Smyth and found it profitable to converse with her on the state of her soul.

17 March 1782
The Select Band at noon was a precious season. Mrs Roberts met with us and all present spoke with freedom and simplicity – I saw a young woman preaching who wept much and took an opportunity to converse with her.

Sunday 31 March 1782 (Easter Day)
Mr Simpson of Kingswood preached this morning and Dear Mr Wesley did not go and I sat with him and had a

profitable season. Dear Mr Wesley preached in the evening from 'Christ is risen indeed'. He showed there was a rational and an experiential evidence of this and how much preferable the latter was to the former ... he gave much encouragement to those who are seeking this faith and to those who have attained, but he did not speak so clearly as in his printed sermons on 'a present Salvation'.

After the preaching was the Love-feast and Glory be to God it was a season much to be remembered. Near 40 made a noble confession – George Braddock spoke humbly and wisely and declared boldly he was cleansed from all sin. Soon after I spoke – and how I was filled with Glory and with God – my whole soul was wrapped up in his presence and in his love. John Booby spoke clearly of receiving Sanctification by faith alone and retaining it 19 years by still acting a momentary faith. He mentioned two women to whom Cousin Robert had been made a blessing – who had long (one of them for 20 years) been seeking a gradual Sanctification from all sin by self-righteous watching and praying etc was, through his word, convinced she never could watch and pray etc in the full gospel sense till she had received a heart from sin set free by faith alone and that to every soul who feels its need 'Now is the accepted time and *now* is the day of salvation'. But as soon as she discovered this she ventured herself on Jesus as a perfect Saviour – and proves he is to her according to her faith. J. Ridgway bore a glorious testimony for God – and declared he received sanctification in a moment by simple faith after striving to sanctify himself for three years together by gradually mortifying every corrupt affection etc. Joshua Norberry, Bill Sharply, etc all declared the same precious truths – that by Grace they are saved through faith – and that from all sin. S. Bradshaw professed Justification, but said he owned he did not experience what he had now heard many profess to do, though a Methodist 20 years.

Mr Wesley got up and said: 'Those who love God with all their heart must expect most opposition from

professors who have gone on for 20 years in a lazy old
beaten track, and fancy they are wiser than all the world
– these always oppose the work of sanctification most.
When John Goostrey spoke Mr Wesley ordered him to
stand on the form that he might be heard – but he was
then so confused he could not say all he intended but
Mr Wesley was much pleased with him and said many
things to encourage the young in years. He said too:
'Some people accuse us of seeking Salvation by works –
they may as well accuse us of playing at Push Pin.[159]
How many have declared tonight that they are saved by
Grace and through faith alone?'

Mr Wesley let the meeting continue two hours which I
never knew him to do before. But his whole soul was
filled with love and thankfulness for so many witnesses
of redeeming love and full salvation'.

Monday 1 April
I went to him at Mr Ryle's and he said 'We had a lovely
meeting last night Hetty, such an evidence cannot be
withstood.'

He met the Select band and it was a precious season.
He called little John Goostrey and desired him to finish
what he was saying last night and to speak freely. John
hesitated a little but then gave a clear account of his
Justification – how he afterwards was convinced of
inbred sin and received sanctification and Dear Mr
Wesley expressed himself much pleased. Molly Rydal
testified she had long sought sanctification in a self-
righteous spirit and that when Cousin Robert told her
you may come as you are, and come now by faith; she
thought he talked nonsense but as soon as she was
convinced of this truth and cast herself by faith on the
all cleansing blood of Jesus – she found he was made to
her sanctification. Ibbe Allen too said she received and
retained it by faith alone and could now in the midst of
trials and notwithstanding many temptations 'Rejoice
ever more – pray without ceasing in every thing'. Ann
Brighouse, Billy Sharply, J. Ridgway, G. Braddock –
Joseph Norberry, P. Goostrey etc all spoke clearly and

wisely and old George Pearson bore a noble testimony. My dear Lord's heart-felt presence peculiarly filled my happy soul.

We breakfasted at Mr Simpson's. Dear Mr Wesley prayed with us and I took leave of him there.

Chapter 18

It is not possible to read Hester's account of the love-feast without feeling a deal of sympathy for 'little John Goostrey'. The prospect of accounting for the state of his soul to his peers must have been daunting enough, but to be ordered to stand on a form and make a declaration of personal faith to the revered leader of Methodism would have brought bolder spirits than John Goostrey to a state of confusion. But for John Wesley if the concept of Scriptural Holiness on the basis of self-accountability did not work in the soul of the likes of John Goostrey, then it was worthless. Wesley is not content to assure him that he is pleased with him, it is important that the nervous young man should express himself and be encouraged to try again in the more intimate atmosphere of the select band on the following morning.

Running through Hester's private diary on John Wesley's Easter visit is a sense of unease about his teaching on instant sanctification. His message in Leek on the subject could not have been clearer: 'I have known a person Justified and Sanctified in an hour.'[160]

Internal disputes within 18th-century Methodism were rare, principally because John Wesley exercised total authority, but Hester is concerned that he is not being consistent and that members of the society are by no means convinced of the truth of his view on the issue. None of these doubts appears in print, nor in the journal as that would smack of disloyalty and that for Hester would be out of the question. Nevertheless there is a need of clarification and Hester struggles to bring herself to question the great man.

Good Friday, 29 March 1782
... some words in this sermon gave me cause to believe he has been warned not to preach on the doctrine of faith and I found a desire to speak to him on the subject – but when I was with him my mouth was shut

respecting it though I found liberty to speak freely and unreservedly on other things.

Easter Sunday, 31 March
... I could not find liberty to request (as I intended to have done) that he would preach on the nature of Faith and a present Salvation though it seemed on some accounts necessary for the sake of those who were prejudiced and though I had entire freedom to speak on any other subject. I see not as yet why my mouth was shut but Lord thou knowest.

Then on the Monday morning she plucks up the courage and puts the point directly to Wesley, although she avoids expressing her own view that might be in conflict with his.

I said: 'Ah sir, there are some who cannot receive all the testimonies that were borne last night, they think those who have been only justified a few months or a few weeks are deceived when they pretend to know anything of sanctification.'

John Wesley is happy to give her a full answer.

Well you and me, Hetty, should not limit God for indeed the time is *now* and will come when a fuller dispensation of the Spirit is given, than has *ever_*been known before. Fifty years ago and before that time there was here and there one instance of the power of God – but it was rarely the case. We seldom heard of Instantaneous Sanctification by faith alone. The Moravian Brethren seemed for a time the most clear, but there is now no people in the world speak so distinct and clear as the Methodists and we now see much clearer than at first and there are more living witnesses of the power of God. I know one Hannah Hooley in this town that was justified at 14 years old and sanctified in about six weeks afterwards and stood firm for about two years and now she is in Abraham's Bosom and you now have several witnesses. I was quite delighted with what that little girl Molly Goostrey, 10 years old, who told me: 'When I felt the love of God and my sins were forgiven – it overjoyed me'.

You and Robert must strengthen the young ones and the new beginners. Robert is very simple and very clear in these things. Joseph must learn of him (I was surprised at this).

I said 'Cousin Robert has been made very useful indeed.' He said 'Yes, he has and he will be, if he continues *simple*.'[161]

Whether Hester ever managed to convince herself and her fellow local Methodists of the truth of this answer is not revealed; evidently these established Methodists were used to working on the faith of the new converts for rather longer than a few hours.

The reference to Robert Roe is interesting. John Wesley held him in high regard, but would not have been impressed if Robert had extended his 'simple' method of preaching into theological speculations in the Oxford mode.

In his sermon in Manchester in 1883, the President of Conference, the Rev. Charles Garrett, looked back at the close fellowship of the early Methodists and painted a glowing picture of their relationship with one another:

They met to talk about their love to God and their love to one another ... They had so much love that their meeting once a month was not enough. They instituted a new meeting – the love-feast – an institution which no other church as yet ventured to adopt.[162]

From the evidence of Hester Roe, Charles Garrett was right to describe Methodism in this way, but it contrasts sharply with what H.D. Rack describes as the 'real vices of Methodists ... jealousy, back-biting and malicious gossip'.[163]

From the moment she stepped into the preaching house for the first time, Hester always expressed her gratitude for the support the Methodist fellowship gave her. What she did not record in her official journal were the less than helpful experiences in the company of senior members of the society, including her cousin Joseph who had been banished from his father's house. Her account of this unattractive side of Methodism can only be found in her private notes.

15 March 1782
I spent the afternoon with Miss Hooley – Mrs Stonehouse was there – but I was tried by the jealousy I saw in the latter.

18 March
S. Bradshaw's class met tonight – having had his class paper returned after throwing it up because his people were barren and did not meet – Mr Roberts gave him some severe hints.

19 March
My dear mother was very severe and a temptation to impatience was darted powerfully twice or three times across my mind – but glory to God I was saved from giving way.

Cousin Joseph was very shy – put on his coat and went out – but returned soon after and asked how I liked his brother (Robert's) sermons etc said he made many mistakes – and I thought spoke in a spirit of bitterness – I was willing to turn the subject – but he would not suffer me and said his brother, when he spoke concerning Christian Perfection, contended much for the Name but seldom insisted on the Nature or fruits – but *he* liked to hear of *those* and that Mr W. – was the best preacher of sanctification in Mr Wesley's Connection.

Not being willing to cavil I answered 'I do not mind who preaches best – if I possess the loving mind that was in Christ' – as he continued to say many things which he knew grieved me and (seemingly with that intention) I thought it best to leave him and come home.

30 March
I had little sleep in the night but was filled with divine love – I arose at 4 – I went to breakfast with dear Mr

Wesley at old Mrs Ryle's. She gave me some rude hints and insinuations respecting my poor health – but I felt a spirit of love towards her.

At nine o'clock he took me and old Mrs Ryle in the chaise with him and we set out for Leek (my mother to my great surprise not opposing it). I answered many accusations Mrs Ryle brought against my cousins in the chaise and dear Mr Wesley seemed well satisfied.

31 March (in the Love-feast)
Cousin Joseph spoke very oddly – said he had met with his greatest trials from professors – the greatest of professors in which he well knew he could hardly allude to none but myself.

The fact that all was not continuing sweetness and light in the relationships between Wesley's preachers and society members is illustrated in the events of August 1783 when Wesley found it necessary to visit Congleton to settle a dispute about the manner in which the Macclesfield Circuit should be divided. His journal entry tells only part of the story.

Saturday 30 August
I heard all the parties face to face, and encouraged them all to speak their whole mind. I was surprised so much prejudice, anger, and bitterness, on so slight occasions, I never saw. However, after they had had it out, they were much softened, if not quite reconciled. [164]

Hester's account of the same incident is far more revealing:

Mr Rogers said –'All I desire is a reconciliation and I appeal to all present if I have not sought it various ways for months past' – Mr Johnson said – 'I never would nor never will be reconciled' the rest seemed more flexible.

At last Mr Wesley got up in much warmth and said – 'You are of your father the Devil – A murderer – and no more in Connection with me – and I will have none connected with me who can deliberately tell me, I will never forgive, etc.' – this had the desired effect. Robert

Johnson fell on his knees – J.L. was near fainting so was J. Roe and Mr Ryle and I wept – God's dear servant then proposed – 'let all henceforth die in oblivion'. All now agreed to it, and shook hands with Mr Rogers who wept tears of joy.[165]

John Wesley's anger might have been real or synthetic. In any event his ability to exercise discipline over his bickering members had its advantages.

Chapter 19

Reference has already been made to the first meeting of Hester Roe and James Rogers at the house of her uncle in March 1781. At that time he was stationed in Sheffield before being appointed for Macclesfield the following year. By then he was already a close friend of both David Simpson and Robert Roe.

The first record of any conversation between Hester and James can be found only in her private diary that reveals a remarkable lack of restraint on the part of a preacher questioning a young lady about her private life and intentions.

> 26 March 1782
>
> I saw Mr Rogers riding into town … I was with Mr and Mrs Rogers alone … he said he wondered I did not marry – I told him I did not know the person whom I could be happy with in that state. He asked: 'Are you sincere with me?' I answered: 'Yes' – 'Well' said he, 'Are you determined never to marry?' I told him I dare not make any absolute determination – I am the Lord's and desire ever to be at *his* disposal – but I am truly happy in my present state – and I see it as a privilege to be free from the cares of a married life and my affections are entirely free – but if God should call me to change my situation I am willing to follow the leadings of his Spirit. He said: 'That is right my dear sister, I would have you marry some time – one like you might greatly add to the happiness of some good man.'[166]

It is most difficult to put diary entries of this kind into a historical context and to judge how appropriate such questions were. But Hester never descends below the level of high spirituality. For her, the priority is the 'leading of the Spirit'; the term 'the happiness of some good man' is that of James not her.

After his father's death, Robert Roe lodged for a while with Hester and her mother, but once he had secured his inheritance from his father's estate, he built his own house which then accommodated all three of them. Benjamin Smith records that 'the house was at once fully consecrated for God' and 'prayer meetings, class meetings and bands were instituted'.[167]

Only nine days after he took possession of his new property, on 9 August 1782, Robert caught a severe cold and died on 13 September. News reached John Wesley in Kingswood on 1 October. 'I read among the letters, in the evening, the striking account of Robert Roe's death; a burning and shining light while alive, but early numbered with the dead.'[168]

Apart from the problems relating to the division of the circuit, settled in spectacular fashion by John Wesley, James Rogers was to be tested by the loss of two of those closest to him, the harrowing experience of the illness and death of his wife, coupled with that of their youngest son, at the beginning of 1784. Martha Rogers was taken ill on 1 January and both she and her eight-month-old baby died on 15 February, leaving James with four-year-old Joseph and two-year-old Benjamin.

The Rev. David Simpson preached the funeral sermon, which was afterwards published as 'The Happiness of dying in the Lord; with an Apology for the Methodists' in which he commented:

> I confess though a clergyman of the Establishment, I see no evil in joining for public worship or social intercourse with any of the denominations of Christians ... I am well aware that this comes not up to the full standard of orthodoxy. But if such a conduct constitutes a bad Churchman, I feel not anxious to be accounted a good one.[169]

Hester's own journal entry relating the events of the first eight months of 1784 is brief.

I had an awful scene to pass through. Dear Mrs Rogers, after the birth of her little James, never recovered her health fully. Mr Rogers being a good deal in the country parts of the Circuit, I was very much with her. At different times she opened her whole heart to me on very tender points, for we were as one soul. For several weeks before her death she entreated me not to leave her when I could possibly help it. O Lord let my end be like hers! I now briefly observe that after many remarkable providences (too tedious to dwell upon here) on 19 August 1784 I was married to Mr Rogers in whom the Lord gave me a helpmate for glory, just such a partner as my weakness needed to strengthen me.[170]

In his account of his life and experience,[171] James Rogers omits to specify the year of his wife's illness and death, thereby failing to disclose that only six months after he buried his wife, Martha, he married Hester Roe. Even in these days it is tempting to think that this was a little hasty. On 14 May 1784, John Pawson sent a letter from York to his friend Samuel Bardsley at the Macclesfield preaching house.

My Dear Brother,
I have lately been to Bristol in order to take my little boy to Kingswood. On my way thither at Birmingham I was told by one of our Preachers that Mr Rogers had lost his wife, but that he would be married again before next Conference. I rather reproved him for being so exceeding rash. He replied, 'I know he will be married to Miss Roe'. I was really grieved to hear him talk so, and dropped the conversation. I thought no more of the matter as I did not believe it, till on my return I called at Sheffield. Here I was told the same thing as before. I answered, it is impossible to be true. I do not believe anything at all about it, and added it is exceeding wrong to be so ready to believe evil one of another. The person replied that the matter was already settled and that there was very good reason to believe that it was in great measure concluded upon before Mrs Rogers died. That it was well known that there had been a very great intimacy

between Mr Rogers and Miss Roe before Mrs Rogers died; that he frequently took her out behind him to the country places and that on one time in particular when Mrs Rogers was to have gone with him, he persuaded her to stay at home and took Miss Roe with him; that Miss Roe was along with Mrs Rogers till she died; that Mr Rogers sent his wife's clothes to Miss Roe three days after his wife was buried, and that they were to be married before the Conference and were to be stationed at Bolton.

I was most heartily grieved to hear this, but could not say it was not true, as I did not know whether it was or not. When I got to Leeds, the next day, I was told the same thing by one that had been to meet Mr Wesley at Manchester and have heard more than enough of it since then. Now my good friend is it possible for all this or any part of it to be true? Can Mr Rogers, can Miss Roe act so imprudent a part? Surely, no; common sense, settling aside religion has taught them to act far otherwise. If the above be true or anything like the truth, in the name of wonder, where is common decency? Where is common prudence? The most carnal people upon earth who have any regard for their reputation will not, do not act in this manner. If this is true how could Mr Rogers write in the manner that I knew he did after his poor wife was dead? I saw one of his letters and if words have any meaning in them, anyone that read that letter would naturally think that he was distressed in the highest degree and almost inconsolable, and I am sure I pitied him from the ground of my heart, as I was then, and still am, labouring under the same most distressing trial.[172]

I assure you these things have made a very great noise indeed and brought Mr Rogers exceeding low in the esteem of those who before were his friends. I hear one speak of it, but with the utmost surprise and abhorrence, sure I am that things of this kind do a very great deal of harm. They really lessen the Preachers exceedingly in the esteem of the people at large. Who can, with any countenance, stand up and pretend to vindicate such conduct, or indeed make any apology for it. For my part, I confess I am ashamed of it, as I must own I look upon it as quite scandalous in a private person and ten-fold more so in a preacher. Lord what is man!

O how careful ought we to be not to give any ground of offence to anyone lest we turn the blind out of the way and make even the Lord's people to transgress. May the good Lord make us examples to the flock not only in word, but in our spirit and temper and our whole conduct.

Pray write to me and let me know the truth of these things.[173]

If John Pawson's letter does nothing else, it demonstrates how quickly news of a spicy kind could spread through the Methodist Connexion.

On the evidence available, it must be conceded that John Pawson had a point. If 'death beds had an almost sacramental function in evangelical experience',[174] then descriptions of deathbed scenes could be described as their related liturgy and it is difficult to share grief in circumstances in which the principal mourner has already lined up a replacement for the deceased.

It is not beyond the bounds of reasonable speculation to believe that Hester consented to a request from Martha Rogers to marry James after her death in order to support his ministry and to look after his children. This may have been so, but suspicions of motives based on more basic human considerations than occupation and domestic duty were enough to promote scandal among the Methodist brothers and sisters.

John Wesley had no time whatsoever for such gossip. As far as he was concerned, the wife of one of his most prominent preachers had died, leaving him with two small sons who needed looking after. Only two things mattered, first that Martha Rogers had died holding a firm Christian faith and second, that James Rogers should get on with his work as soon as possible. If the dying Martha had made a private arrangement with Hester to marry her husband soon after her death, it made practical sense and social convention meant nothing to John Wesley. On 7 November 1784, he wrote to Mrs Sarah Crosby:

The case of Hetty Rogers was widely different. I know more of it, beginning middle and ending, than most people in England. And I am clear that, first to last, she acted in good conscience toward God and man. As things stood, it was not a sin for her to marry, but a duty; and to marry when she did. And never was any one woman so owned of God in Dublin as she has been already.[175]

For Wesley, death was a matter for celebration and grieving, if it was absolutely necessary to grieve, could be decently over in a few hours. In the meantime there was work to be done in Ireland that would take the newly-married couple away from the tongue-waggers for a while, but they would be back; the Stationing Committee comprised John Wesley and he would see to it.

Chapter 20

It is inconceivable that Hester and James Rogers should have married in such haste without the blessing, even permission, of John Wesley, although there is no record of a meeting with them or of correspondence between them on the subject. Hester may well have married out of a sense of duty, the word used by Wesley in his letter to Sarah Crosby, and if this was a view he put to Hester, it would have been quite enough to bring her to a quick decision. That he would not hesitate to give advice is evident from his letter to Mrs Jane Cock expressing concern that marriage to an unapproved spouse might render her less 'useful' as a Christian.

> Dublin, 7 April 1789
> I cannot but say, that it was some concern to me when I first heard that you were married, because I was afraid that you would be less useful than you might have been in a single life. And indeed, I hoped that if you married at all it would have been to one of our Preachers. Then I could have stationed him in some circuit where I should have had frequent opportunities of conversing with you.[176]

What effect all this controversy had on the local Methodists is not known. To a degree, the reputations of Hester and James were sheltered by the dominating influence of John Wesley as he continued to tour the Connexion, but the protection was not complete and the so-called 'scandal' had a lasting effect on their relationships within Methodism.

It may be significant that David Simpson attended the Leeds Conference of 1784 at Wesley's invitation, but it is not known if the occasion was used, at least in part, to muster support for the Rogers, temporarily exiled across the Irish Sea. It is much more likely that he had been recruited to speak in favour of the Deed of Declaration which had been drafted by William Clulow, a native of Macclesfield who was a personal friend of Simpson.

James Rogers was a Yorkshireman, born in Marsk in the North Riding in February 1749. Like Hester, he had a Christian upbringing and there was a remarkable similarity between her adolescent convictions on the relationship between ethics and accountability and those of neighbours of the Rogers visiting James' father to discuss matters of religion.

> I remember one night in particular, many queries were proposed about salvation: none of them thought it possible that any certainty could be attained in this life, whether they should be saved at last or not. But the general opinion was, that our actions would all be weighed in the day of judgment; and if our good deeds over-balanced our bad ones, we should go to heaven; but if the contrary then we should go to hell. But some dissented a little from this, and thought, 'Nay, But God was merciful, and had sent His Son to die for sinners and that their best way would be to amend their lives, and do all they could, and Christ would make up the rest. One of these, they all agreed, must be the way; and, to confirm them in this conclusion, one observed that the parson of the parish was exactly of the same mind.[177]

The life of James Rogers both as a local and travelling preacher had its challenging times. On one occasion he and a number of his Methodist friends were violently assaulted in a village near Whitby and he almost drowned in the course of a missionary visit from his appointment circuit at Edinburgh to the Isle of Bute.

Like Hester he was greatly impressed by the character and presence of the Rev. John Fletcher. In 1777 he was appointed to minister in the east of Cornwall and during the 500-mile journey from Edinburgh he took the opportunity to visit the great man during a break at Bristol.

... he came towards us with arms spread open, and eyes lifted up to heaven. His apostolic appearance, with the whole of his deportment, amazingly affected us. The first words he spoke, while yet standing in a stable by his horse, were a part of the sixteenth chapter of John, most of which he repeated. And whilst he pointed out the descent of the Holy Ghost, as the great promise of the Father, and the privilege of all New Testament believers, in a manner I never had heard before, my soul was dissolved into tenderness, and became even as melting wax before the fire.

Before the small party left, John Fletcher administered the sacrament;

A sense of the Divine presence rested upon us all; and we were melted into floods of tears. His worthy friend, Mr Ireland, grieved to see him exhaust his little strength by so much speaking, took him by the arm, and almost forced him into the house, while he kept looking wishfully, and speaking to us, as long as we could see him ... We then mounted our horses and rode away. That very hour more than repaid me for my whole journey from Edinburgh to Cornwall.[178]

When James Rogers married Hester Roe, he already had an impressive track record as an evangelist, a necessary qualification for anyone facing the challenges of a ministry in a troubled Ireland.

By 1784 the lay leadership of English Methodism particularly in the industrial north, was dominated by families of a new middle class whose antecedents were anything but wealthy. In his *Further Appeal* to the clergy in 1745, John Wesley was quite frank that he had little or no interest in preaching to the upper classes; 'the rich, the honourable, the great, we are thoroughly willing to leave to you'[179] and J.D. Walsh links extracts from three of the hymns of Charles Wesley which emphasise the low esteem in which the brothers held those of high estate -

> The rich and great in every age
> Conspire to persecute their God
> Our Saviour by the rich unknown
> Is worshipped by the poor alone
> A rich man saved. It cannot be
> But by a more abundant grace.[180]

Hester had frequently heard David Simpson preaching on the same theme and come to her own decision to cut herself off from family connections which would have given her material advantages in life.

But Ireland was not England and evidence of the truth of David Hempton's statement that,

> whereas in England Wesley saw himself as having a special, but not exclusive, ministry to the poor, and frequently made barbed criticism of the worldliness of the English church and its gentry patrons, in Ireland his mission worked downward from the gentry class and outwards from the garrison in a way that would have been unthinkable in England,[181]

can be found in John Wesley's journal as early as August 1747.

> Between six and seven I went to Marlborough Street. The house wherein we then preached was originally designed for a Lutheran Church, and will contain about 400 people; but four or five times the number may stand in the yard. Many of the rich were there and many ministers of every denomination.[182]

This simply would not have happened in England at that time. The following April he preached at Tyrell's Pass:

> In the evening many of the neighbouring gentlemen were present, but none mocked. That is not the custom here; all attend to what is spoken in the name of God. They do not understand the making sport with sacred

things; so that, whether they approve or no, they behave
with seriousness.[183]

So when Hester and James Rogers arrived in Dublin, they
found themselves in a Methodist society which had a tradition
of supporting and associating itself with an establishment
which was alienated from the vast majority of poor people in
the Roman Catholic community. The divide between Catholics
and Protestants ran deep so that each side adjusted even the
facts of the past to suit its own historical perspective. For
example, John Wesley was quite prepared to accept the
grossly exaggerated account by the British Master of the Rolls,
Sir John Temple, of the Irish Massacre of 1641.

> I procured a genuine account of the great Irish massacre
> of 1641. Surely never was there such a transaction
> before, from the beginning of the world! More than two
> hundred thousand men, women and children butchered
> within a few months, in cold blood, and with such
> circumstances of cruelty as makes one's blood run cold!
> It is well if God has not a controversy with the nation,
> on this very account, to this day.[184]

Wesley was frustrated that 'at least ninety-nine in an
hundred of the native Irish remain in the religion of their
forefathers. The Protestants, whether in Dublin or elsewhere,
are almost all transplanted lately from England';[185] not that
he approved of a manner of government which relied on the
constitutional oppression of 'Penal Laws and Acts of
Parliament'.[186] Ireland in the 18th century was seething with
discontent and E.H. Nolan described the breaking out of the
Irish Rebellion in 1798 as 'the smouldering embers of
disaffection bursting forth into a flame'.[187]

This was a dangerous place for travelling Methodist
preachers with a commission and a zeal to evangelise among
the whole community regardless of allegiance. After his third
visit to Ireland, John Wesley wrote to a friend that, 'the Irish
in general, keep no bounds. I think there is not such another
nation in Europe so impetuous in their love and their hate.
That any of the Methodist preachers are alive is clear proof of

an overruling Providence, for we know not where we are safe.'[188]

There is considerable irony in the fact that the highly intelligent and literate Mrs Hester Rogers was suddenly faced with charge of the ladies of a Methodist society whose husbands held high office in government and commerce, yet she was, initially, estranged from her potential converts among the poor by a political and religious divide.

She was by no means impressed by their first hosts, a Dublin solicitor and his wife. She described their visit as an 'unprofitable season' and later protested about his 'trifling and ridiculous conversation'.[189]

Hester's time was a precious commodity and she could use it for better purposes than for frivolous chatter. When she and James were taken down the coast to one of his preaching appointments in a new luxury boat, fitted internally with mahogany, she wondered, 'Can this make the owner happy? Alas no! It cannot be unless his soul were first adorned with Christ, and made meet for God.'[190]

These diary extracts give the impression that Hester was having difficulty in adjusting to a life of ministry away from her own town. This was far from the case. In her autobiography, she summarises their record in a few words:

> We were gladly received and the Lord gave us the hearts of the people. Our hands being thus strengthened by the Lord, we agreed solemnly to devote ourselves and our all to him and his work. And, all glory to his name, we saw a blessed revival. In three years the society increased from about five hundred to eleven hundred and upwards; and we had good cause to believe about four hundred were converted to God.[191]

She wrote to the Rev. John Fletcher in December 1784 reporting a situation of near Utopia in which 'Stewards, Leaders and people all unite and have only one stroke – how they may best promote each other's happiness and the cause of God'.[192]

That is as much as 19th-century Methodists were allowed to know about the Rogers' ministry in Dublin. The statistics are impressive, but it was by no means the whole story.

Chapter 21

Rumour, especially that based on false information, has a nasty habit of spreading quickly, and where people's reputations are at stake stories about suspected wrongdoing tend to grow in the telling. John Pawson's letter, written three months before the Rogers were married, contains allegations of a kind which had no foundation in fact, and Wesley's reference to the truth being 'widely different' from the information Sarah Crosby had received suggests that by October gossip had stretched the truth beyond all reason.

When news of the episode reached Hester's closest friends, Elizabeth Ritchie and Sally Salmon, who was staying with Elizabeth at Otley near Leeds, they must have been hurt and perplexed. Those who thrive on malicious gossip relish the prospect of revealing every salacious detail to those nearest the people involved and Sally wrote what must have been a most difficult letter to Hester repeating at least part of what she had been told. She also asked if she could visit Dublin for a while, no doubt to give support to her long-standing friend.

Hester could have replied in a few sentences, setting the record straight and suggesting that the proposed visit should be deferred until the spring when the weather would be better and it would be more convenient to arrange accommodation. She could have, but she did not. Instead she used the opportunity to reveal many of the problems she had to face in her first year in Dublin, coupled with an account of remarkable success in the expansion of the work of Methodism in the district. Despite her difficulties, on which she does not dwell, Hester maintains a full confidence in her faith and even manages to thank God for what she has suffered.

Dublin, 6 August 1785

My Dear Friend

To receive a few lines from you after so long a silence gave me real pleasure, believe me I always valued your friendship and sincerely desired your welfare in all things and at all times since I first knew you. I can make much allowance for your being staggered at the various things laid to my charge knowing well the subtlety of your informers and I hope, my love, you will hereafter put more confidence in the veracity of a friend who, however accused, you *never* proved unfaithful. All glory to my God alone. I well knew he would make my innocence appear and I praise him for all I suffered. Already he hath rewarded me tenfold. Be assured I love you my dear Sally as I ever did or do and will pray for you and I know the God of love will answer. But let me know all the particulars of your state and I can do it far better and tell me, what shall I ask? 'ready are you to receive, ready is thy God to give'.

But I have a painful task in writing what follows. When Mr Wesley wrote to dear Miss Ritchie and when I wrote last I did hope and promised myself much happiness in seeing you both in Dublin in a few weeks. But as things have fallen out I think it my duty simply to inform you of the real truth rather than suffer you to come so far under so many inconveniences and when God seems to shut up your way, especially as you desire me to advise you freely I have made it a matter of much prayer and find I can act no otherwise though it is a greater cross that I have had to take up since I came to Dublin. But I believe infinite wisdom sees it good for me that my will should be crucified and that a cross should be intermixed with by numberless blessings, which truly are multiplying every day – O that I may improve them! But I must come to your point When I mentioned to several friends after Mr Wesley left us that I expected Miss Ritchie and you they appeared quite disconcerted and told me they were very sorry and hoped I would write to prevent your coming till next summer, for they themselves, and they know it to be the case with others, had gone to the utmost their circumstances would allow in expenses on Mr Wesley's account and other occasions of pressing necessity and can do no more this summer, whereas whenever <u>you</u> come they would wish to treat you with every possible respect having heard from me much respecting you, so that every family would invite you by turns with 30 or 40 friends to meet you, in order to make your coming an extension of blessing. But the peculiar disposition of the Irish is such that unless they could do this they would not make you welcome at all – perhaps many of them would never come where you were. This is the temper of our Dublin friends in particular – this they plainly told me and there is no turning them – again there is no possibility of receiving you at present. In our house we have only two beds and the maid is obliged to sleep in the kitchen (not like our kitchens in England) – for one week, indeed, we left our own bed entirely for dear Mr Wesley – but you can hardly conceive the inconvenience it put us to, but he on his return , he slept at Mr Keens our Steward's though a mile distant from the preaching house and though he did all his business with us in the day and had to walk every morning at five o'clock. The same family, our Stewards, would gladly receive you and I depended on their now doing so – but a family from the North is coming very shortly to stay with them for some months so that they will be quite full and much harried, having five children at home, the eldest seven. Another on whom I depended, a lady of piety and fortune, is gone into the country for her health for some months. Mr William Smith also is much displeased at his wife inviting you before the opening of the new chapel and declares he will not receive you till then. I could not wish you to be here as, first, you would be put to the painful alternative of not attending the chapel and by your example doing real hurt to the cause of Methodism – or giving such offence to that family as would not easily be forgiven and you would find the winter season in Dublin very inconvenient and disagreeable. At Mr Smith's you could see us and the Methodists only very seldom – for our people will not invite them or their visitors except for three or four families and you would not find means of doing the good you wish and neither you not I could bear the walks backward and forward.

Again Mrs Smith speaks very disrespectfully of dear Miss Ritchie in letters from England to her mother who has read them to several – insinuating that she is too highly thought of and too much set up and that it has hurt her and puffed her up – this grieved me a good deal though I know my friend too well to believe it and convinces me of what I before believed that Mrs Smith is not truly united to those who profess Christian Holiness. Her heart is with the Calvinists and Mrs E. says it is wholly her ordering that Calvinist Methodists are to preach in the chapel.

All these things, however, put together I think my dear friend you will see with me that your call is not to Dublin this summer. Yet I hope to see you while we stay and it appears to me next April or May (but no later by any means) will be the time you may return *with us* after the Dublin Conference. Surely your way will then be open. If good for us I know it will – though some providences are very mysterious – we know our Jesus hath done all things well and his wisdom transcends ours. O may my will be ever lost in his.

Glory be to the Triune God of life – he is increasingly precious to my soul every day. I am often overwhelmed with his goodness, so that my ravished soul tastes the bliss of those around his Throne and constantly I feel 'His Presence makes my Paradise and where he is Heaven'. O my love, how does he help, strengthen, comfort and lead the weakest, the unworthiest of all. How graciously condescends to my minutest wants, Yea, as the Poet says: 'And numbers every sacred hair – As I remained his single care!'

Glory, Glory, Glory to the Father, Son and Spirit for evermore. His gracious work still goes on amongst us here. Thirty three have joined the Society, all awakened and stirred up to seek the Lord since dear Mr Wesley left us – about four are also justified as are many fully renewed. Three weeks ago after Mr Rogers had been preaching there was an abundant outpouring of the Spirit and when he ceased praying the people refused to go and he was constrained to sing and pray again. One, if not more, was justified and at our Band Love-feast was a wonderful effusion of Divine Love. I believe not one soul was untouched – one told us God set his soul at liberty and I expect to hear of several more.

Mr Wesley divided all the classes and we had some fears it should cast a damp on the work but I believe it will not. I never knew such a number of people so quickly give up their own will. There are now 45 classes, 21 more than we found. My dearest partner, thank God, is increasingly happy. Often our eyes fill with tears of divine love together and our hearts with unutterable gratitude to an indulgent God and we daily, on our bended knees together, praise him. In him we are united as one heart and a heartfelt sense of his approving smiles heightens our enjoyment of each other – makes our happiness as complete as it can be in a transitory fleeting world – and blissful thought, we are hastening to its eternal completion in the presence of our God.

Now, my love, permit me to beg you will write soon and urge dear Miss Ritchie to do the same, to whom my sincerest love. If I don't hear from you soon I shall think I have grieved you by forbidding you to come.

You may tell Mrs Smith I have advised you not to come so late in the summer to Dublin so that I think the way will be open next Spring – but do not read her my letter or tell her any more of its contents. I have written in confidence of real friendship, which I hope you will ever find in me my dear Sally.

You truly affectionate

Hester Ann Rogers[193]

It will be noted that Hester does not even begin to justify her decision to marry, justification is a matter of faith and lies within the soul. It is enough that her motives have been pure and if her friend has had less than full confidence in her 'veracity' then that is a matter for her to sort out. No other explanation is deemed necessary.

Hester is entirely open in expressing the happiness she has found in her relationship with her husband and considers there is no need to apologise for it. For her, divine love extends into human love and raises it to a far higher level than can be experienced by mere emotion.

Much later, James would assert that religion, 'by refining love, increases both its fervour and constancy'.[194] But Hester recognises the 'transitory nature' of human relationships and, as always, her thoughts are never far from heaven.

Chapter 22

Action prompted by feelings was a concept alien to the rationalistic thinkers of the mid 18th century, but assurance of salvation was the stimulus for the evangelical activity of early Methodism, set out in poetic form in many of the hymns of Charles Wesley, sometimes in a single sentence; 'My heart is full of Christ and longs its glorious matter to declare.'[195]

Hester had used similar language on the morning after her conversion. 'My mother was astonished at the change which appeared in my countenance and my whole deportment and I soon told her the happy cause – that I, a poor sinner, had received forgiveness ... 'I see an eternity of him before me. O that you knew what I feel'.[196]

The journal entries of Hester Roe prior to her marriage are concerned almost exclusively with her search for holiness. Life with one of John Wesley's preachers brought responsibilities of a more practical kind with a greater opportunity for active evangelism and this is reflected in her writings.

Their ministry in Dublin is summarised as 'three successful years'.[197] Her own contribution to this success can be gauged from her letter to the Rev. John Fletcher when they had been in Ireland for less than four months.

Dublin, 14 December 1784
Two weekly classes are committed to my care, one with 38 members and the other with 36. Within the last quarter 10 of those have received a sense of pardon. I have also undertaken a class of young girls, from nine to 14 years of age. Since we arrived four months ago we have certain accounts of 46 justified, 8 sanctified and 100 added to the society. On 18th November we had a love-feast. We know of nine that we have reason to believe were justified and many lukewarm professors were stirred up. Two of these found peace the week after.[198]

When John Wesley next visited Dublin he was clearly impressed:

6 April 1785
I found such a resting-place at our own house as I never found in Ireland before: and two such preachers, with two such wives, I knew not where to find again'.[199]

No doubt when he took the Rogers' bed, he put his head on the pillow and quickly fell asleep, unaware of the 'inconvenience' raging elsewhere in the building. However, it should be noted from Hester's letter that when he returned to Dublin after he had toured Ireland, he took advantage of alternative accommodation, despite the long early morning walk, so as not to further complicate the domestic routine of the overcrowded house.

What impressed John Wesley most when he returned to Dublin was that the increase in membership had been maintained. 'I feared very many of the society would be lost before my return, but I found only three. So that 737 of them remained'.[200]

A more complete record of the ministry of Hester and James Rogers in Dublin than can be found in the journals of either John Wesley or Hester was written by James. The most significant sentence in this account is the one that denies 'any appearance of what is commonly called wildfire ... The work was not only gradual, but deep'. This was the spreading of scriptural holiness in full measure.

I had not been many days in that city before I saw some fruit of my labour, and was fully satisfied that my going there was of the Lord. A few years ago there had been a sifting time in the society. But the troublers of Israel were now removed, and we found the people fully prepared to receive the Gospel of peace. Within the space of six weeks several found mercy, and returned public thanks to Almighty God for a sense of his pardoning love; and many more were deeply awakened.

This we received as a token for good and the hopes of all were encouraged to expect a more glorious outpouring of the Spirit. For this a general spirit of supplication was given, and the Lord answered for Himself in a wonderful and glorious manner. At the quarterly love-feast on Sunday 10 October, soon after the people began to speak their experience, a poor woman under deep conviction cried aloud for all present to pray for her. We all instantly fell on our knees, and entreated the Lord on her behalf. In that moment the power of God descended in such a manner, that I believe not one unaffected soul remained under the roof. We continued wrestling in prayer for nearly half-an-hour, and afterwards found not less than seven souls were clearly justified, and many who had received notes of admission on that occasion were deeply awakened, and immediately joined the society. The next evening another was justified under the word, and two more under the last prayer, when also a poor backslider felt that the Lord had healed him. Within the next week following five others were brought into Gospel liberty; and in the month ensuing 13 more. At a love-feast held in our Gravel-walk chapel eight persons received a sense of pardon, two backsliders were restored and a stranger, who had got admittance for that time, was truly awakened.

About a fortnight after this we had our band-feast when two more were justified and three professed to be at the same time renewed in love. In the beginning of December one was justified at St Patrick's Church when receiving the sacrament; and one who had been educated a Roman Catholic, but was awakened six weeks before, received a sense of pardon under the word in our preaching house; as did two more, who were convinced of sin at one of the above-mentioned love-feasts. On Christmas Day our chapel at Whitefriars was well filled at four o'clock in the morning. We continued in preaching, exhortations and prayer till eight. It was a remarkable season and the power of God was manifest in the whole congregation. I cannot ascertain the exact number of souls that were converted to God, but several found a clear sense of His pardoning love shed abroad in their hearts; and many others were awakened who had remained until that time entirely strangers both to God and His people. The first Sunday in the new year all the society, with several other friends, assembled together to renew their covenants with God. It was a most solemn season. I seldom remember to have felt more of the Divine presence at any time. The language of my heart, and I believe of most present, was – 'How awful is this place! Surely it is the house of God: this is the gate of heaven.' So it was found to be: three penitents and two backsliders were at that blessed ordinance reconciled to God by faith in the blood of Christ. And on Thursday and Friday evenings following, while the form of the covenant was farther explained, four more received forgiveness of sins; and two others under the preaching on the ensuing Sabbath. From that time to 25th March 36 more received a sense of pardoning mercy.

On Good-Friday two more were justified under the word and one at the communion in St Patrick's on Easter-Day many could witness, 'Christ is risen indeed'. Two received a sense of pardon in the morning and in the evening four more felt the power of Him who bruised the head of the serpent while attending to a sermon delivered from Genesis iii 15; and, beside these, three others were blessed with a degree of inward liberty they had not known before. We had reason to hope our honoured father, Mr Wesley, would have spent Easter with us, but being detained in England longer than he expected, he did not arrive in Dublin until April 11th before which time three more were pardoned, two backsliders were restored and two others experienced the great truth, 'the blood of Jesus cleanseth from all sin'. Mr Wesley spent about a fortnight in the city during which time eight persons were justified under his preaching; and before he returned from visiting the country societies, 15 souls found peace with God.

In the time of our Conference two others received a sense of pardon and three more were enabled to believe to full salvation. The whole number of souls brought into the glorious liberty of the children of God in the course of the past year were 130; and an increase in the society of 200 members, after excluding all those whom we judged improper to remain.[201]

On 15 February James Rogers' assistant died of fever, leaving him as the sole full-time preacher, but even this tragedy did not stop the work of expansion.

But the death of a preacher so much loved had a good effect on the people; we cried to the Lord and he was better to us than all our fears; and, great as my fatigue was, my health grew better; so did the Lord perfect His strength in human weakness. I was led to consider this was the Lord's work and that He could carry it on with or without means or by what instruments He chose. The congregations continued very large and the prayer-meetings and classes exceedingly lively; scarcely a week passed in which some were not awakened and joined to the society; and frequently under the word, or at other ordinances, three four and five would be found to praise God for His converting grace ... The number of persons whom we had reason to believe were savingly brought to the knowledge of God among us in the course of the second year, was 178 souls, which is 48 more than in the former year; and the society amounted to more than 900 members.

Having had so considerable an increase, and for so long a time together, it was natural to expect according to the common course of things the tide would now begin to ebb. But He who is able to do above all that we can ask or think still continued to awaken sinners in great numbers. Zion's cords were lengthened and her converts flowed in from every quarter.

Several concurring circumstances induced Mr Wesley to comply with the request of the society in leaving me amongst them another year; and I was favoured with a fellow-labourer of piety, integrity and good abilities; nor did the Lord give us less fruit than before. When we came to deliver up our charge at the yearly Conference, after thoroughly weeding the classes, and lopping off 126 members, some for immorality and others for omitting to meet their class, yet the society had increased to 1136; which made in all an addition of above 600 souls in three years; and from the best accounts we could keep, we had every reason to believe 458 of these were savingly converted to God.[202]

Omitted from the account of James, but included in the appendix to Hester's 'Experience' is a reference to an attempt to assassinate him while he was preaching on 7 November 1786. Fortunately the gun of the would-be assassin jammed.[203]

In 1787 Hester and James Rogers were moved to Cork, but before James took up his appointment, it was necessary for them to travel to Macclesfield to settle some outstanding personal affairs there.

Chapter 23

In the late 18th century all journeys by sea were hazardous and the voyage across the Irish Sea was no exception. On 11 July 1787, John Wesley chartered the *Prince of Wales* to take him and his party of preachers with their families, including Hester and James Rogers and the Rev. Dr Thomas Coke, who had arrived in Dublin a few days earlier after a month-long journey from Philadelphia, to Parkgate in Cheshire.[204] They nearly did not arrive there.

> At seven we sailed with a fair, moderate wind. Between nine and 10 I lay down, as usual, and slept till nearly four, when I was awakened by an uncommon noise, and found the ship lay beating upon a large rock about a league from Holyhead. The captain, who had not long lay down, leapt up and, running upon the deck when he saw how the ship lay, cried out, "Your lives may be saved, but I am undone!" Yet no sailor and no woman cried out. We immediately went to prayer, and presently the ship, I know not how, shot off the rock and pursued her way, without any more damage than the wounding of a few of her outside planks. About three in the afternoon we came safe to Parkgate.[205]

Hester and James travelled on to Macclesfield where her mother 'received us with great affection',[206] which, in the circumstances, was hardly surprising. Mrs Roe was probably far more aware of the perils of living in Ireland than Hester would ever have allowed herself to acknowledge and here was her daughter with her husband, two stepchildren and her only grandson, James, born a year earlier, bearing the Christian name of her dead husband. After Conference at Manchester, they travelled back to Dublin and then, after a week's stay, to Cork to take up a new appointment.

Methodism had been established in the city in the face of continuous opposition, punctuated by outbreaks of mob violence, such as on one occasion at the end of May in 1749 when John Wesley was told, 'I had no place there yet, it being impossible for me to preach now, while the rioters filled the streets'.[207] However, by 1785 the situation had calmed down and Wesley was free to speak in the open-air.

Sunday 8 May
In the afternoon I stood in the vacant space near the preaching-house, capable of containing many thousands. An immense number assembled. There was no disturbance: the days of tumult here are over; and God has now of a long season made our enemies to be at peace with us.[208]

It would not last long, but at least there was a pause before the violence resumed. James Rogers attributed a setback in the welfare of the society the previous year to 'unhappy jarrings'[209] that had reduced the membership from about 500 to 397.

Success in the ministry of the church cannot properly be assessed in terms of membership statistics, yet once again the societies in the charge of Hester and James Rogers gained momentum on an impressive scale.

We added a hundred to the society before New Year's Day; and have reason to believe upwards of 60 of these were converted to God. But the progress of the work did not stop here; the Lord continued to prosper His word to the salvation of many souls in that city. And it is probable more good would have been done but for a few troublesome spirits, who under a pretence of standing up for the Church, hurt the minds of many. The Lord greatly blessed His word among the soldiers. Eight sergeants and about 40 privates met constantly in class, and some of them became eminent for piety. Notwithstanding every difficulty cast in the way, the society increased to 660; many of whom were much alive to God, and ornaments to their profession when we left.[210]

Three weeks into the New Year of 1788, Hester reported to John Wesley that there had been further progress

Cork, 24 January
The number of classes is increased from 24 to 36 and 56 souls have found peace with God since September last. The Christmas festival was a most blessed season. On Christmas morning at four o'clock, the preaching house was well filled. My class now being divided I meet 20 on a Tuesday and 18 on a Friday. My heart is knit to these precious souls.[211]

Some years later Dr Thomas Coke explained how Hester used the Methodist class meeting system as a means of evangelism.

Mr Rogers, on entering a circuit, would only give very few to her care, desiring her to complete the class out of the world; and soon, by her conversation and prayers, and attention to every soul within her reach, would the number spring up to 30 or 40; and then her almost cruel husband in this respect would transplant all the believers to other classes and keep her working continually at the mine.[212]

Hester deemed pregnancy and childbirth scarcely worth a mention in her journal and they were not allowed to interfere with the work of God. 'Confinement', if the word is not totally inappropriate, was a matter of hours rather than days or weeks and had to fit into the hectic schedule of evangelism and class meetings. To the responsibilities of Joseph, Benjamin and James was added that of nurturing a new baby, John, born in their last year in Cork. The pressures of illness could be testing, but, according to the journal, only had the effect of strengthening faith and commitment.

At the time of a severe nervous fever the cloud was only a few days; and that I believe was merely owing to the body; for though in a week afterwards all the feelings of nature were touched, I felt nothing contrary to resignation, patience or love. At the time I now speak of my own recovery was doubtful. Mr Rogers (oppressed with grief through my illness and by his attention to me day and night) was very ill. James had a worm fever; the maid confined with sickness; and my little John, six weeks old, lying in convulsions for three days. Surely in this scene the Lord magnified his power in supporting my weakness, and enabling me to say 'Good is the will of the Lord'. After this season my consolations were abundant; and my faith, love and communion with God much deepened.[213]

Hester and James Rogers acted as hosts to John Wesley when he visited Cork in 1789. On an earlier visit to Ireland he had expressed his disapproval on discovering that services at five o'clock had been discontinued for almost 18 months. Evidently some 30 years later, discipline had been restored to the scheduling of the first meeting of the day, but another matter of concern had arisen;

Monday 4 May
... at five, when I endeavoured to quench the fire which some had laboured to kindle among the poor, quiet people, about separating from the Church. In the evening, I preached on Luke viii 24 and the word was as fire; it pierced to dividing of soul and spirit, joints and marrow.[214]

The sermons may have quenched the fire of separation for a while in Cork, but the subject would cause considerable distress to Hester and James Rogers when John Wesley was no longer alive to deal with it.

Chapter 24

The scale of the success of the ministry of Hester and James Rogers in Ireland was exceptional, even at a time when Methodism was expanding rapidly, and this was not unnoticed by its leader. Hester had

> some encouraging letters from Mr Wesley. In the last two, he mentioned his intention of removing us to London at the ensuing Conference. I trembled at the thought of so important a charge, but committed it to God in much prayer.[215]

According to established protocol, James Rogers should have been informed of his appointment before his wife knew anything about it. However, as the 'Stationing Committee' had been corresponding privately with the lady for the previous 14 years, the normal rules of procedure were waived. It is inconceivable that James would have taken offence; he was far more concerned about the nature of the challenge facing him. 'I should have objected to the appointment only I was afraid of running counter to the order of God'.[216] It seems the decisions of John Wesley in these matters were regarded as being blessed with divine authority.

> It was the intention of the 1790 Conference that James Rogers should accompany Wesley on his almost daily journeys and assist him in his services, whilst his wife cared for the house in City Road, with its busy life, from early morning until 10 o'clock at night.[217]

According to one editor of Wesley's journal, 'Hester Ann was not equal to the strain of such a preacher's house, especially when Wesley himself was in residence, because she was no longer the strong north-country woman whom Rogers married in Macclesfield'.[218] By no stretch of the imagination could Hester ever have been accurately described as 'strong', the reason for her inability to run the City Road manse was that she had become pregnant again and weaker with each succeeding pregnancy.

The services of Miss Elizabeth Ritchie as housekeeper were called upon 'believing it to be my providential path, I entered on my new engagement and found sufficient business on my hands'.[219] 'Sufficient business' soon involved nursing John Wesley in his last days before he died on 2 March 1791.

Death as the gateway to eternal bliss was the ultimate experience of 18th-century Methodists so that the deathbed scene of the leader of the Methodists was of particular significance. Elizabeth Ritchie was asked to keep a journal to record events and Hester used her own considerable literary talents to describe Wesley's final moments.

To be with that honoured and much-loved servant of God for five months, and then to be witnesses of his glorious exit, was a favour indeed. But O, how awful the scene! – how unspeakable the loss. The solemnity of the dying hour of that great, good man, I believe, will ever be written on my heart.

A cloud of the divine presence rested on all; and while he could hardly be said to be an inhabitant of earth, being now speechless, and his eyes fixed, victory and glory were written on his countenance and quivering, as it were, on his dying lips! O could he then have spoken, methinks it would have been nothing but Victory! Victory! - Grace! Grace! – Glory! Glory! No language can paint what appeared in that face! The more we gazed upon it, the more we saw of heaven unspeakable! Not the least sign of pain, but a weight of bliss. Thus he continued, only his breath growing weaker and weaker, till without a struggle or a groan, he left the cumbrous clay behind, and fled to eternal life in the bosom of his faithful Lord.[220]

As John Wesley passed away, James Rogers read these words:

> Waiting to receive thy spirit,
> Lo! The Saviour stands above,
> Shows the purchase of his merit,
> Reaches out the crown of love.[221]

The death of Wesley greatly affected James Rogers.

> ... it is impossible to describe what I felt on the removal of our venerable father to paradise: yet I esteem it the greatest honour ever done to me, that I was providentially called to accompany him in his last journey and be with him in his latest moments.[222]

It is likely that John Wesley had brought James Rogers to London because he was an effective preacher and model pastor who would quickly make an impact on the capital city for the Methodist cause. This he did:

> It is a matter of praise that the great Head of the church is still with us in a powerful manner. Many are the souls that have been convinced and brought God amongst us, in and near this city, in the space of 18 months past. The congregations are large and attentive; and the societies are increased to upward of 3,000 members, which is more by some hundreds that they ever were before.[223]

Had James been free to devote the whole of his time and energy to preaching and pastoral work, he would have avoided much of the stress he had to endure in the period immediately after the death of Wesley. Managing the affairs of Methodism had never been easy, even for a benevolent despot such as John Wesley with an iron will to exercise his authority whenever he deemed it necessary,

John Wesley, as one of the founding fathers of Methodism, had the status to act in this dictatorial manner at a time when authority was rarely challenged, but his death coincided with the dawn of a new age. The concept of democracy as a political and social philosophy was anathema to Wesley who was convinced that government exercised through the will of the people would only result in further restriction of freedom. After all, human nature was fundamentally evil so only evil could come from collective will. But the people of America had already successfully rebelled against the authority of the British crown with the declared objective of establishing a democratic system of government and the revolution raging in France had similar aims, even though it was turning increasingly violent.

In this climate it was only natural that there should be growing pressure from societies to influence the future of Methodism. It might have helped if the destiny of Methodism had been established but it had not. John Wesley had remained an ordained priest in the Church of England to his dying day, but his preaching houses were registered as dissenting chapels to give them legal protection. There was no common ground in the thinking of the membership at large with many Methodists continuing to regard themselves as loyal members of the Established Church and others, with little or no connection with the Church, pressing for complete separation.

There were those in Methodism who would have relished the prospect of taking over full authority in the wake of Wesley's death, but James Rogers was not one of them. He was used to exercising spiritual guidance over his flock, either directly or through his class leaders, not joining or leading conspiracies of those prepared to fight for supremacy through intrigue and procedural manipulation. This dedicated and sensitive man found the whole episode distasteful, especially as it followed immediately upon the death of his leader.

> Added to this irreparable loss, many other disagreeable circumstances, arising from the general stir occasioned through our whole Connexion by this awful event, made the situation of my brethren and me very distressing. God alone knows how my own mind was exercised from the time of Mr Wesley's death until the Conference.[224]

At such a testing time James Rogers could count on the support of his wife as witnessed by Dr Thomas Coke:

> When he was stationed in London his steady attachment to the Methodist discipline raised up many powerful enemies against him. His sufferings were inexpressible, and his constitution very much impaired thereby. Mrs Rogers was, to my knowledge, his support indeed. More true conjugal love could not, I think, be manifested by a wife to her husband.[225]

It is sad that Methodism, struggling to establish its identity in a new era, should have inflicted such strain on two of its most loyal servants. Hester puts a brave face on it and, as always treats trouble as a challenge for faith to overcome.

> When I look back on the trying scenes we have passed through since this awful event, and consider we are yet monuments of grace and saving power, I am lost in wonder and in love. Mr Rogers, in particular, has been tried in the fire, and exposed, through his office, as a mark to shoot at; yet, through infinite mercy, I believe he will come out of it all the more purified.[226]

Although James had been willing, albeit reluctantly, to answer the call of duty, he had felt a deep frustration that he would have been more constructively engaged elsewhere:

> Before I left home to preach the Gospel, I thought an itinerant life was calculated above all others, to promote a growth in grace, as it cuts all pecuniary advantages and secular concerns. I still believe God is able to uphold His messengers, and cause his grace to abound towards them. But, upon the whole, few are more critically circumstanced, all things considered, than a Methodist preacher: especially those who are called to superintend in our Connexion. It is a mercy indeed, if while these are looking to their Lord's vineyard, they do not neglect their own. I often fear this has been too much my own case; and have heartily wished I had less to do with public affairs in the church of God, and that I might spend the whole of my time in recommending the love of Christ to perishing sinners.[227]

In a relationship as close as that between Hester and James Rogers it was inevitable that she would be affected by his weakened physical and mental condition: '... these trying exercises of my dear partner have been keenly felt by me. And my nervous system, weakened by that dangerous fever at Cork, has also greatly suffered by these things; which like wave upon wave, have followed each other.'[228]

There were those in Methodism at that time who had reason to be ashamed of themselves.

Chapter 25

The manner in which James Rogers conducted himself in the service of Methodism from the time of Wesley's death in 1791 until the Manchester Conference of that year was at least appreciated by his fellow preachers, who used the occasion to grant him a unanimous vote of thanks for his 'exertions and his immovable patience and fortitude in defence of Methodism'.[229] Having survived the ordeal of keeping Methodism united, on a temporary basis at any rate, he was happy to return to the work for which he was better suited and record that 'the people in general are at peace, and the word of the Lord continues to run and is glorified'.[230]

In the meantime Hester's health was failing. Added to her worries about her husband were the strains of the death of her second son, John, and further pregnancies resulting in the births of three daughters, Mary, Martha and Hester, in quick succession. James was stationed in Spitalfields and to Birmingham the following year in the hope that the move away from London would help Hester recover her health.

In July 1794 she decided to accompany her husband to the Conference in Bristol as a means of visiting Kingswood School to see her eldest son, James, and her step-sons Joseph and Benjamin. By then, she was six months into yet another pregnancy, her sixth. The journey involved an 18-hour coach drive from London to Bristol, which was virtually suicidal for someone in her condition and fragile state of health.

Hester was well aware that she was not likely to survive the perils of another childbirth. She had never been afraid of the prospect of her own death, but she knew only too well the pressures and responsibilities this would place on James when she was no longer there to support him. She hoped he would find consolation in the poem she composed a few days before she went into labour.

My hour is come, and angels round me wait
To take me to their glorious happy state;
Where, free from sickness, death and ev'ry pain,
I shall with God in endless pleasure reign.
Transporting thought! Thou dearest man, adieu!
I feel no sorrow but in leaving you.
O thou, my comfort, thought and only care,
In these last words thy kindness I'll declare.
In truth, in constancy, in faithful love,
Few could you equal, none superior prove.
Compell'd by frequent sickness to complain,
You strove to lessen and assuage my pain,
A tender care you never failed to show,
A constant sharer in my present woe.
More, I would say, my gratitude to own,
But breath forsakes me, and my pulse is gone.
      Adieu, dear man – O spare
Thy flood of grief and of thy health take care
My blessing to my babes! Thou wilt be kind
To the dear infants whom I leave behind.
Train them to virtue, piety and truth,
And form their manners early in their youth,
Farewell to all who now on me attend,
The faithful servant and the weeping friend
The time is short till we shall meet again,
With Christ to share the glories of his reign.[231]

Hester survived for only one hour after the birth of the last of her children and marshalled every last drop of energy to praise the Lord she had served so faithfully all her adult life. Her words were recorded:

The Chariots of Israel and the horsemen thereof are all waiting to carry me home ... He cries 'Arise my love, my fair one, and come away'. Amen, saith my willing soul ... My soul is on the wing ... How welcome the stroke that shall break down these separating walls, knock off my fetters, throw open my prison door and set me at liberty. Angels surround my bed to carry me away. I come, I come, blessed messengers of my God! Haste and convey

117

me to his beloved embrace! A foretaste now I feel! Nay, so am I filled with glory and with God, that more I could not bear and live! Oh may I ever feel the sacred flame and through eternity proclaim the depth of Jesus' love! Amen and amen![232]

Her funeral sermon on 26 October 1794 at Spitalfields Chapel, London, was preached by the Rev Dr Thomas Coke who could speak from his personal friendship with her about her qualities and work for the kingdom of God:

"Her maternal care and affection shone bright. Though she devoted much of her time to religious duties in public and private, yet nothing seemed to be left undone which could make her children comfortable and happy. She was equally, nay, if it were possible, more attentive to Mr Rogers' children by his former wife than to her own. To the whole of them she delighted to give 'precept upon precept, line upon line, here a little and there a little' watering the whole of her labours upon them with many tears and daily fervent prayers.

As a friend she was faithful and immovable in her attachments: nothing but her friends forsaking God could induce her to abate her love for them. She was formed for society and possessed the most delicate feelings which could arise from social principle. And when some of her dearest intimates treated her with neglect on account of some disputes in the Connexion, which they had nothing to do with, she could still weep and love and pray for them, not as unworthy of her friendship or of the favour of God, but as led away from her by misinformation and error of understanding, and perhaps also by some deviations from the perfect love of God.

But her forte, her greatest excellence, consisted in her enjoyment of God. A very considerable part of her life evinced that salvation from sin and salvations from sufferings are very different things. Her firm patience under deep afflictions has been rarely, if ever, exceeded. Her conduct in the hour of nature's sorrow, in every instance, astonished all who were near her; all her sufferings on these occasions were very exquisite .She hardly ever in her life was in what is generally termed low spirits. She was ever cheerful, never light; and always ready to lift up the hands of her husband and her friends, and to encourage their hearts. She enjoyed for many years that glorious blessing which St John, in the fourth chapter of his first epistle, speaks as of his own experience, and that of many of whom he was writing, that 'perfect love' which 'casteth out all fear that hath torment'. In short she walked with God, she lived in the blaze of Gospel day, and Christ was to be her all in all.

And as a public person, she was useful in a high degree. She never, indeed, assumed the authority of teaching in the church, but she visited the fatherless and widows in their affliction, and delighted to pour out her soul in prayer for them. Very many dying persons entered into the liberty of God's children under her prayers and exhortations; for she possessed a peculiar gift in bringing a present salvation home to the soul. The profit received in Macclesfield from her holy conversation for years before she married, induced pious and mourning souls to visit her; and a very considerable part of her time was daily spent in answering cases of conscience, spreading forth loveliness and excellencies of Christ to penitents, and in building up believers in their most holy faith. She was a leader of classes and bands and a mother in Israel to the young believers entrusted to her care.

Thus did the Lord mould this blessed woman into his image, as the potter does his clay, and use for his glory, as the writer does his pen, until she had served him in her generation and he said to her, It is enough, come up higher."[233]

Chapter 26

In his study of 18th-century prose, J.A. Hammerton distinguishes between the charm of the style of literature and its claims as a vehicle of instruction. It is Hammerton's opinion that in the final analysis 'prose lives because of its power, not for its prettiness', but his claim that 'charm and distinction are peculiarly characteristics of our 18th-century prose,[234] is relevant to any study of the writings of Hester Ann Rogers. Her English is breathtaking in its beauty and in expressing his admiration of it, John Wesley was not resorting to flattery. James Rogers refers to his wife as having received a 'pious and liberal education from her childhood'.[235] The piety was learned from the father to whom she was devoted and the rest came from Adlington. The historical context matters. Hammerton quotes Sir Edmund Gosse's summary of the importance of the period in the development of our language; 'The century found English prose antiquated, amorphous, without standard or form, it left it a finished thing, the completed body, for which subsequent ages could do no more than weave successive robes of ornament and fashion.'[236]

Hester was able to express herself in a style of high quality after absorbing the best that writers of the 17th and 18th centuries could offer. Reference has already been made to the expansion of the library at Adlington during the time of Charles Legh. This is of far greater significance than the apparent self-indulgence of a country gentleman spending his fortune on books to impress his friends and acquaintances. This was part of an active process of the bringing together of the greatest works of literature and setting standards for future generations to follow. These volumes and manuscripts now rest in the Portico Library in Manchester, to which the collection was sold in the 19th century, and their scale and importance can only be understood from a scrutiny of the 1830 inventory.[237]

David Avery

T. Pratt devotes a whole chapter of his book on the Portico
Library to the former Adlington Collection and how it relates
to England in the 18th century.

The whole varied life of this romantic period of wigs and
swords, artificial manners and loose morals is revealed
in this valuable collection now known as the 'Adlington
Pamphlets'. These pamphlets had been collected with
great labour by Mr Legh and, undoubtedly, both he and
his agents must have been indefatigable in their efforts
to have gathered together so comprehensive a collection
of publications relating to the 18th century. The
collection is particularly rich in plays, and includes
such literary treasures as first editions of Goldsmith
and Sheridan with more than 1200 individual items.[238]

The works of William Shakespeare had been virtually
ignored for over 100 years until the 1740s, yet nine volumes
of his plays and poems, printed in 1714, had come into the
possession of Charles Legh at Adlington.

Hester's birth in 1756 clearly places her as a child of the
European Enlightenment, confirmed by the inventory of an
Adlington library that is dominated by the philosophical
works of John Locke and his successors and the books of
sermons of the Latitudinarians who portrayed God as wise
but remote, ruling the world in the harmony of an ordered
universe. In this climate, Christianity was no longer seen as a
religion of mystery with God revealing himself to the
individual hearts of men and women, in marked contrast to
the convictions of those in the Evangelical Revival, including
the Methodists, who stressed the value of religious experience.
No trace of conventional theology can be detected in the
published sermons of the Rev. George Whitfield, preaching to
the miners of Kingswood, near Bristol, in the earliest days of
the Evangelical revival:

O my brethren my heart is enlarged towards you. I trust
I feel something of that hidden, but powerful presence of
Christ while I am preaching to you. Indeed, it is sweet, it
is exceedingly comfortable. All the harm I wish you is

that you felt the like. Believe me, though it would be hell to my soul to return to a natural state again, yet I would willingly change states with you for a little while, that you might know what it is to have Christ dwelling in your hearts by faith.[239]

In his review of one of the first Methodist hymn books, published in 1753, Maldwyn Edwards spells out the manner in which the hymns of the Revival broke from the cultural and religious climate of the Enlightenment.

There is a defiant smashing of all the canons of the classical school. The theology of experience could not be narrowly contained within the polished couplets of the Augustan age. It needed for its turbulent emotion every known variety of metre and some not hitherto employed. It was the harbinger of the Romantic Revival for it was instinct with feeling and it joyfully recognised the infinite worth of the ordinary man.[240]

E.H. Carter describes the coming of the Romantic Revival as a 'return to nature',[241] but it was more than this and D.W. Bebbington identifies the movement as being 'well fitted to be a vehicle for religious thought' with its leading characteristics of 'emotion and imagination, with a consequent emphasis on moments of intense experience.'[242] Charles Wesley includes a central place for emotion in many of his hymns;

Thrice happy I am
And my heart it doth dance at the sound of His name.[243]

Hester Ann Rogers expressed herself with the clear objective of exploiting her own literary talents to spread the gospel through her own testimony and she was at her most effective in her letters, particularly those to her cousin, Robert, in his Oxford college. Her disciplined Augustan prose is entirely consistent with the style of the English Enlightenment, but she shares the mysticism of Charles Wesley and strict rationality never stands in the way of vivid expressions of religious ecstasy. Her mood is much nearer to that of William Blake than that of Alexander Pope.

John Wesley always linked the pessimism of the doctrine of original sin to the power of the Holy Spirit to raise the souls of humanity to match that of God himself. Goethe accepted the same concept of human potentiality in his fight against the restrictions of Isaac Newton's scientific laws, particularly those relating to light: 'Light – not the light passively received by the eye but light emitted by the eye – this was indeed god like ... were God's own power not inherent in ourselves, how could divinity enchant us?'[244]

Hester witnesses to the truth of the argument, takes it to its triumphant conclusion in describing the nature of spiritual renewal on her own soul and stamps her distinctive Christian mark on Romanticism.

Chapter 27

Those anticipating that a study of the writings of Hester Ann
Rogers will in some way relate to issues which find their way
on to contemporary church agendas through the influence of'
proliferating special interest groups and the 'politically correct'
will be disappointed. Her only recorded comment about
national affairs concerns the military threat from France in
the wake of the French Revolution and appears in her journal
entry for 19 February 1794.

> Having heard much of late respecting public manners
> and about an expected invasion, with all its
> consequences, I have been led to much secret prayer ...
> I received an answer 'There shall no evil befall thee,
> neither shall any plague come near thy dwelling'.[245]

This assurance from Psalm 91:10 is less than a
comprehensive assessment of Europe in political and military
turmoil, but it is entirely consistent with Hester's application
of her faith to any impending calamity in accordance with the
specific advice given to her by John Wesley in his letter of 11
February 1779:

> It is a great mercy that, on the one hand, you have
> precious warning of the trials that are at hand and on
> the other, are not careful about them, but only prepared
> to encounter them. We know indeed that these, as well
> as in all things, are ordered by unerring wisdom, and
> are given us exactly at the right time, and in due
> number, weight and measure. And they continue no
> longer than is best, for chance has no share in the
> government of the world. The Lord reigns, and disposes
> all things, strongly and sweetly, for the good of them
> that love him'.[246]

Hester's determination to defy the fierce opposition of her family in maintaining her Methodist connection illustrates the truth of J. Wolffe's point that: 'Evangelicalism could be a potent emotional and spiritual resource in stirring a woman's heart to assert her own identity.'[247] Beyond that, it offered her, as it did all other women, 'the concept of spiritual equality with men'.[248] This is short of any claim that she was in some way challenging the structure of authority within a Methodism that was vested in a male-only Conference dominated by John Wesley. Methodism reflected the patriarchal society in which it operated, but many of the classes and most of the bands were segregated according to sex so that the leaders of the women's groups exercised almost total control over their proceedings. Even then, responsibility for the soul did not rest with the leadership, male or female, but within the individual and spiritual maturity brought a level of dignity, recognised by both men and women in Methodism and by others outside it, which was frequently totally at odds with status in society at large; not that status mattered to Hester, 'others may boast of riches and estates, their high birth and parentage'.[249]

What is the verdict of history on Hester? The answer will never be definitive because the Evangelical Revival and those connected with it made such an impact on the social and political life of the country that views can only be subjective and vary according to the stance of the historians concerned. In her extensive study of emotional and gender issues in early Methodism, Dr Phyllis Mack summarises the conclusions of a host of secular writers who have criticised the movement.

> In different ways each of these scholarly traditions promoted an image of the ordinary Methodist as a person without autonomy or agency: terrified of damnation, mesmerised by charismatic preachers, hysterical in public worship, imitative of conservative bourgeois values, enslaved to an inflated work ethic and emotionally repressed in intimate relations.[250] ... secular historians need an angle of vision that allows them not only to accept spiritual concerns as sincere and legitimate, but to share, however imperfectly, the

struggles of ordinary Methodists and lay preachers to
stand with individual men and women as they worked to
share their own subjectivity, not in a single cathartic
moment in a revival meeting, but over a lifetime.[251]

After her death, Hester, who fails to meet any of these
secular criteria except that of a highly developed work ethic,
could only have been established as a role model if the
hallmarks of her faith and witness had conformed to the
Methodist pattern based on justification and new birth. She
had the ability to express these concepts in the form of a
personal testimony. When she asks John Wesley for guidance
in explaining the nature of Assurance and Christian
Perfection to Robert Roe, he neither takes on the
responsibility himself nor resorts to the use of the technical
language of theology at his disposal. Instead, he simply
advises her to be her own witness.

> ... sanctification is plainly set forth in Scripture. But
> certainly before the root of sin is taken away, believers
> may live above the power of it. Yet what a difference
> between the first and the pure love! You can explain this
> to Mr Roe by your own experience. Let him follow on
> and how soon may he attain it![252]

Later John Wesley pays tribute to the constancy of her
developed faith and, again takes care to link conviction with
personal witness:

> So very few retain the same ardour of affection which
> they received either when they were justified, or when
> they were sanctified. Certainly none need to lose any
> part of their light or their love. It may increase more and
> more. Of this you are a witness for God.[253]

Two centuries later, the potential interest in and value of
Hester's recorded experiences will depend to a large extent on
the theological stance of the reader. Hester's testimony is
probably capable of inspiring only those whose faith is rooted
in the Wesleyan heritage, inside Methodism and elsewhere.

Those who reject any concept of a need for redemption as proclaimed by the New Testament will find no support in the journal or letters of Hester Ann Rogers. The argument that Christian discipleship simply combines a duty to worship with a flexible social ethic and leaves morality as a matter for individual choice was well known to her and it was practised by an overwhelming majority of her contemporaries, whose conduct was as far away from scriptural holiness as it was possible to get.

Sadly, the writings of Hester Ann Rogers are not likely to be published in their entirety. This is a pity. Her 'sainthood' stemmed from a decision made shortly after her death to extract from her journal and letters only those elements that related to her spiritual experience and to exclude virtually everything else. In the early 1980s, Paul Wesley Chilcote researched the thousands of pages of the manuscript journal and discovered that it

> not only provides countless insights regarding the nature of the Methodist movement and the organisation of the Societies during those crucial years [of the late 18th century], but also affords a glimpse of the mature Wesley as viewed through the eyes of this sensitive lay woman.

Chilcote considers it unfortunate that 'almost all of the material dealing with Hester's relationship with Wesley from their first meeting in 1776 to her marriage ... in 1784 was deleted from the original and all subsequent editions' of her works.[254]

When extracts from Hester's journal were first published, John Wesley had only been dead for five years and such was his status that it may have been feared that any change of focus in his direction would have undermined the objective of projecting the nature and depth of Hester's spirituality.

The recorded story of any 'saint' will always comprise edited highlights of the person's life. After using the phrase 'our own Methodist saint', Rosa Gladding compares Hester with St Catherine of Sienna, whose parents tested 'the reality of Catherine's call to a devout life by putting her to all the most laborious tasks of the house'.[255] It is much more likely that the patience of Mrs Roe had been tested to breaking point by her daughter's insistence on pursuing her own version of a 'call to a devout life' than for any nobler motive on the part of the lady. Nevertheless, if Hester's ordeal could be related to that of an established saint, it would do her reputation no harm to mention it.

To modern minds, editorial selection does nothing to enhance Hester's standing. 19th-century Methodists had their own reasons for looking back to a 'golden age' with its individual heroes and heroines, but it is reassuring for us to know that these giants of the Methodist Revival frequently felt isolated and unpopular, even among their own kind. There is reason enough to marvel at and celebrate Hester's literary artistry in its own right, but full knowledge of the context in which she was writing presents new generations with special inspiration and challenge. Her faith was tested by the harsh realities of opposition, persecution, a weak constitution, frequent ill health, the dangers of childbirth and malicious gossip, but these adversities were not allowed to stand in the way of her witness or her outstanding success as an evangelist.

Chapter 28

Its white-hot convictions, poured into the hearts of the first adherents, cooled down and became crystallised codes, solidified institutions, and petrified dogmas ... The impetuous missionary torrent of earlier years was tamed into a still flowing rivulet and eventually into a stationary pond.[256]

D.J. Bosch is lamenting the fate of the early church not that of Victorian Methodism, but his tone is remarkably similar to that of Hugh Price Hughes in 1883, comparing the state of his church to that of the panic-stricken Elijah, sitting under his juniper tree. According to Bosch: 'every religious group that started out as a movement and managed to survive did so because it was gradually institutionalised otherwise it would have disintegrated: this is simply a sociological law.'[257] But other influences had been at work in the 19th century that had nothing to do with the laws of social science. The resolve of Hugh Price Hughes to chop down the 'accursed juniper tree of Methodism'[258] coincided with the Victorian 'crisis of faith' which stemmed from intellectual objections to the whole fabric of Evangelical doctrine with Original Sin as its foundation. Biblical authority was increasingly regarded as being in conflict with the discoveries of science that offered the prospect of a better world through human effort, not religious faith. In this climate many considered it absurd to conceive of God as

> creator who sentenced many of his creatures to eternal punishment and who required an innocent victim's suffering to appease his wrath; in short, the traditional doctrines of hell and substitutionary atonement were themselves under moral judgment.[259]

The Methodist Church was not unaffected by this line of thinking. Towards the close of the century, several tutors in its theological colleges regarded early Methodism's view of sin and redemption at best as quaint and it its worst as outdated and irrelevant. This coincided with lay leadership of the denomination being dominated by respectable members of the middle class who had been nurtured in God-fearing families and who had maintained high moral standards in public and private life. Their loyalty to their Church was not in question, but it was easy enough for many of them to pay lip-service to established creeds and restrict attention to Methodism's convictions about corrupt human nature to the ritual singing of Wesley hymns.

By the time the first edition of *Joyful News* came into print in February 1883, its editor, the Rev. Thomas Champness, was already part of a movement that had recognised the symptoms of spiritual lethargy and taken action to cure it:

> The years that are past can tell enough of hours wasted in sleep or idleness, while the plough has been left in the unfinished furrow, and the precious grain, which might have been 'seed for the sower and bread for the eater', has been devoured by the fowls of the air. Thank God, there are already signs of a glorious season.[260]

Hugh Price Hughes specifies the nature of the action: 'Thank God, those miserable days have passed away. Instead of sitting under that wretched juniper tree, Methodism is now conducting revival missions and putting forth her enormous strength for the evangelisation of England.'[261]

Our perception of late Victorian Methodism matters less than that of its own leadership and its President scarcely disguised the fact that in his opinion it suffered by comparison with its own past. So in encouraging a new generation of Methodists to 'carry out and compete the work of Methodism' Charles Garrett urges them to look for inspiration to the zeal and courage of a Yorkshire stonemason, John Nelson, and for an illustration of 'holiness of heart and life'[262] to Hester Ann Rogers. His pleas may well have prompted the further reprint of her *Experience and Spiritual Letters* two years later in 1885.

Then the link between the past and the present, crucial to our understanding that in looking to their roots, the late Victorians were not indulging in collective nostalgia.

D.W. Bebbington identifies that other link between holiness and revivalism, illustrated by the fact that 'the leading Wesleyan connexional evangelists of the 1880s, Thomas Cook, Thomas Waugh and Edward Davidson, were all preachers of entire sanctification'.[263]

So, one of the distinctive legacies of John Wesley to 19th-century Methodism was his teaching on holiness and those Methodists of 1883 who were anxious to know what scriptural holiness meant in practice were invited to read the testimony of Hester Ann Rogers; she was the role model.

End notes

[1] J.D. Walsh lecture, Open University course, 'Evangelicals, Women and Community in 19th-century Britain', 1992.

[2] Andrew Worth, 'From Fame to Obscurity,' in *Bulletin of the Wesley Historical Society*, London and Home Counties Branch, Spring 1993, p. 19.

[3] J.D. Walsh, Open University lecture, op. cit.

[4] Ibid.

[5] K. Gnanakan, *Kingdom Concerns*, 1993, Inter-Varsity Press: Leicester, p. 67.

[6] G. Walgreen, *Silk Town Industry and Culture in Macclesfield, 1750-1835*, 1985, Hull University Press, p. 140.

[7] Hester Ann Rogers, *Experience and Spiritual Letters*, 1885, T. Woolmer, p. A3.

[8] Ibid., p. 6.

[9] Ibid., p. 6.

[10] Ibid., p. 5.

[11] Ibid., p. 7.

[12] Ibid., p. 8.

[13] Ibid., p. 9.

[14] Ibid.

[15] Ibid., p. 10.

[16] Ibid., p. 15.

[17] Ibid.

[18] Ibid., p. 9.

[19] Richard Brinsley Sheridan, *The Rivals*, 1883, Routledge and Sons: London, p. 87.

[20] Hester Ann Rogers, op. cit., p. 13.

[21] C. Morrison, *Macaulay*, 1882, London, p. 69.

[22] H.D. Rack, *Reasonable Enthusiast: John Wesley and the Rise of Methodism*, 1992, Epworth Press: London, p. 1.

[23] C. Stella Davies, *A History of Macclesfield*, 1968, Manchester University Press, p. 185.

[24] Hester Ann Rogers, op. cit., p. 15.

25 C.F. Legh, *Adlington Hall*, 1978, English Life Publications: Derby, p. 2.

26 C.F. Legh, *The Organ at Adlington*, 1978, H. Oldfield and Son Ltd: Macclesfield, p. 4.

27 C.F. Legh, *The Organ at Adlington*, op. cit., p. 11.

28 Ibid.

29 Hester Ann Rogers, op. cit., p. 15.

30 Ibid., p. 213.

31 Ibid., p. 13.

32 Ibid., p. 16.

33 W.H. Challoner, Lancashire and Cheshire Antiquarian Society, 1950–1, vol. 1, p. xii,

34 Asa Briggs, *A Social History of England*, 1994, Weidenfeld and Nicholson: London, p. 194.

35 *JWJ*, op. cit., vol. v, p. 36.

36 Hester Ann Rogers, op. cit., p. 15.

37 Rev. John Gaulter, *Memoirs of the Rev. David Simpson, MA, Minister of Christ Church, Macclesfield, 1775-88, friend of Wesley*, 1799, p. 1.

38 D.W. Bebbington, *Evangelicalism in Modern Britain*, 1994, Routledge: London, p. 139.

39 Gaulter, op. cit., p. 1.

40 Rev. David Simpson, *Sermon on Useful and Important Subjects*, 1774, T. Bayley: Macclesfield, p. 47.

41 Ibid

42 Robert Roe, *The Arminian Magazine*, 1783, p. 522.

43 Hester Ann Rogers, op. cit., p. 17.

44 Rev. D. Simpson, op. cit., p. 161.

45 Ibid., pp. 228–9.

46 Hester Ann Rogers, op. cit., p. 20.

47 Rev. D. Simpson, op. cit., p. 231.

48 Hester Ann Rogers, op. cit., p. 17.

49 Ibid., p. 19.

50 Ibid.

51 Ibid., p. 20.

52 Rev. David Simpson, op. cit., pp. 203-4.

53 Hester Ann Rogers, op. cit., pp. 22-3.

54 Ibid., p. 23.

55 Ibid., p. 24.

56 Ibid., p. 20.
57 Ibid., p. 25.
58 Ibid.
59 *JWJ*, op. cit., vol. vi, p. 14.
60 Ibid.
61 Benjamin Smith, *History of Methodism in Macclesfield*, 1875, p. 18.
62 Ibid.
63 Ibid.
64 *JWJ*, vol. iii, p. 224.
65 Ibid.
66 Ibid., p. 299.
67 Rev. B. Smith, op. cit., p. 33.
68 Ibid., p. 34.
69 *JWJ*, vol. vii, p. 256.
70 Robert Roe, *Arminian Magazine*, 1783, p. 522.
71 Hester Ann Roger, op. cit., p. 28.
72 Ibid.
73 Ibid.
74 Ibid., p. 17.
75 E.P. Thompson, *The Making of the English Working Class*, 1968 Victor Gollancz: London, p. 285
76 Ibid. Thompson notes that the 'Welsh Jumpers' are 'Cousin to the American Shakers'.
77 *JWJ*, op. cit., vol. vii, p. 153.
78 Benjamin Smith, op. cit., p. 65.
79 G. Walgreen, op. cit., p. 139.
80 Charlotte Bronte, *Shirley*, quoted by Marsh Wilkinson Jones in *Proceedings of the Wesley Historical Society*, vol. li, Part 5, May 1998, p. 163.
81 J. Wolffe, *Evangelicals, Women and Community in 19th century Britain*, 1994, Open University: Milton Keynes, p. 25.
82 J, Wolffe, op. cit., p. 17.
83 D.W. Bebbington, op. cit., p. 5.
84 H.D. Rack, op. cit., p. 343.
85 Rev. D. Simpson, op. cit., p. 104.
86 Ibid., pp. 115–16

[87] D.L. Watson, *The Early Methodist Class Meeting*, 1985, Nashville Discipleship Resources: Nashville, p. 126.

[88] *JWJ*, vol. i, p. 151.

[89] Hester Ann Rogers, op. cit., p. 88.

[90] Ibid., p. 28.

[91] Rev. John Wesley, *Forty-Four Sermons*, reprinted 1980, Epworth Press: London, p. 53.

[92] Ibid., p. 57.

[93] Ibid., p. 61.

[94] D.W. Bebbington, op. cit., p. 8.

[95] Hester Ann Rogers, op. cit., p. 31.

[96] T. Shenton, *Forgotten Heroes of the Revival*, 2004, Leiminster Day One Publications, p. 106.

[97] Rev. David Simpson, op. cit., pp. 233–4.

[98] *The Methodist Magazine*, January 1813. pp. 10–11.

[99] Rev. J. Gaulter, op. cit., p. 1.

[100] Gaulter's mistake is repeated in printed editions of Wesley's journal including that of Nehemiah Curnock, 1909, vol. vi, p. 142, fn. 2.

[101] J. Ritson, *The Romance of Primitive Methodism*, 1909, Edward Dalton: London, p. 138.

[102] J.D. Walsh, Lecture, op. cit.

[103] Ibid.

[104] G. Walgreen, op. cit., p. 163.

[105] A. Worth, op. cit., p. 19.

[106] Rosa E. Gladding, *Wesleyan Methodist Magazine*, February 1913, pp. 137–8.

[107] *Wesleyan Methodist Magazine*, 1824, p. 475.

[108] Silk History Group, *Bridge Street*, 1998, Friends of Macclesfield Silk Heritage, p. 14.

[109] This building now houses the Macclesfield Silk Heritage Centre with a room specifically dedicated in memory of David Simpson.

[110] Hester Ann Rogers, op. cit., p. 57.

[111] A. Worth, op. cit., p. 20.

[112] G. Malmgreen, op. cit., p. 166.

[113] A. Worth, op. cit., p.

[114] Rev. Paul Smith, *Whatever Happened to our Raison D'Etre?*, 1997, Headway Conference Lecture, p. 3.

115 *JWJ*, op. cit., vol. i, p. 476.
116 *JWJ*, vol. vi, p. 100.
117 *The Letters of the Rev. John Wesley, M.A.*, ed. John Telford, 1931, Epworth Press: London, pp. 255–6 (hereafter *Letters*).
118 Hester Ann Rogers, op. cit., p. 50.
119 Ed. John Telford, letters, op. cit., p. 256.
120 Ibid.
121 Ibid.
122 Ibid., p. 258.
123 John Banks, *Nancy, Nancy*, 1984, Wilmslow Penwork: Leeds, p. 42.
124 H.D. Rack, op. cit., p. 268.
125 Ibid., p. 257.
126 John Telford (ed.), *Letters,* op. cit., p. 261.
127 Ibid., p. 263.
128 Ibid., p. 259.
129 Hester Ann Rogers, op. cit., p. 82.
130 Ibid., p. 99, 15 May 1778.
131 Ibid., p. 107.
132 Ibid., p. 113.
133 Ibid., p. 134.
134 Ibid., p. 136.
135 Andrew Worth, op. cit., p. 20.
136 Benjamin Smith, op. cit., p. 143.
137 *JWJ*, vol. vi, p. 293.
138 Benjamin Smith, op. cit., p. 158.
139 Hester Ann Rogers, op. cit., p. 62.
140 Ibid.
141 Benjamin Smith, op. cit., p. 163.
142 Hester Ann Rogers' manuscript diary, John Rylands University Library, Manchester, vol. ii, ref. C340, p. 172.
143 *JWJ,* vol. vii, p. 346.
144 Mr Aeneas MacLardie's daughter married Dr Jabez Bunting, the most prominent Wesleyan Methodist leader in the first half of the 19th century.
145 Hester Ann Rogers' manuscript diary, op. cit., vol. ii, pp. 172–3.
146 *JWJ*, op. cit., vol. vi, p. 346.

[147] Rev. J.B. Dyson, op. cit., pp. 19–20.
[148] Ibid., p. 17.
[149] Rupert E. Davies, *Methodism*, 1976, The Garden City Press: London, pp. 81–2.
[150] Hester Ann Rogers' manuscript diary, op. cit., vol. ii, pp. 173–6.
[151] D.L. Watson, op. cit., p. 118.
[152] Ibid., p. 67.
[153] Ibid., p. 120.
[154] Ibid.
[155] Hester Ann Rogers, op. cit., p. 54.
[156] H.D. Rack, op. cit., p. 187.
[157] D.L. Watson, op. cit., p. 2.
[158] Hester Ann Rogers' manuscript diary, op. cit., vol ii, pp. 170–2.
[159] 'Push Pin' was a popular table game,
[160] Hester Ann Rogers' manuscript diary, op. cit., vol. Ii, p. 176.
[161] Ibid.
[162] Rev. Charles Garrett, *Joyful News*, 22 February 1883, p. 2.
[163] H.D. Rack, op. cit., p. 436.
[164] *JWJ*, vol. vi, p. 443.
[165] Hester Ann Rogers, op. cit., vol. iii, p. 101.
[166] Hester Ann Rogers manuscript diary, op. cit., vol. ii, p. 173
[167] Benjamin Smith, op. cit., p. 188.
[168] *JWJ*, vol. vi, pp. 373–4.
[169] A, Worth, op. cit., p. 19.
[170] Hester Ann Rogers, op. cit., pp. 62-3.
[171] Thomas Jackson (ed.), 'Life of James Rogers' in *The Lives of the Early Methodist Preachers*, republished 1998, Tentmaker Publications: Stoke-on-Trent, vol. ii, pp 435–472
[172] The wife of John Pawson had died on 9 December 1783. He remarried on 12 August 1785.
[173] J.C. Bowmer and J.A. Vickers (eds), *The Letters of John Pawson*, 1995, Methodist Publishing House: Peterborough, vol. i, p. 23.
[174] D. Rosman, 'Faith and Family Life,' Offprints Collection, Open University course.

175 J.C. Bowmer and J.A. Vickers (eds), op. cit., p. 23.
176 T. Jackson (ed.), *The Works of the Rev. J. Wesley*, 1872 (3rd edition), London, p. 87.
177 T. Jackson (ed.), 'Life of James Rogers', op. cit., vol. ii, p. 437 (hereafter 'Life of James Rogers').
178 Ibid., pp. 453–4.
179 T. Jackson (ed.), *The Works of the Rev. J. Wesley*, op. cit., p. 239.
180 J.D. Walsh, 'Elie Halevy and the Birth of Methodism' in *Transactions of the Royal Historical Society*, 1975, 5th series, vol. xxv, p. 37.
181 David Hempton, *Evangelism in English and Irish Society, 1780-1840*, Oxford University Press, 1982, p. 41.
182 *JWJ*, op. cit., vol. iii, p. 313.
183 Ibid., p. 346.
184 Ibid., p. 314.
185 Ibid.
186 Ibid.
187 E.H. Nolan, and E. Farr, *History of England*, 1859, vol. iii: 'From the Accession of George III. to the Twenty-Third Year of the Reign of Queen Victoria'. James S. Virtue: London, 1859, p. 293.
188 *JWJ*, op. cit., vol. iii, p. 486.
189 Hester Ann Rogers, op. cit., p. 212.
190 Ibid., p. 245.
191 Ibid., p. 68.
192 Ibid., pp. 138–9.
193 Hester Ann Rogers manuscript diary, op. cit., p. 482.
194 E. Rogers, *Experience and Spiritual Letters of Mrs H.A. Rogers*, 1885, T. Woolmer: London, Supplement p. 237.
195 Charles Wesley, *The Methodist Hymn Book*, 1972, The Garden City Press Ltd, p. 244.
196 Hester Ann Rogers, op. cit., p. 332.
197 Ibid., p. 68.
198 Rev. John Fletcher and his wife had visited Dublin in 1783 and this could be the reason why Hester Rogers reported progress to him. *JWJ*, op. cit., vol. vii, p. 258.
199 Ibid., p. 66.
200 Ibid., p. 94.

201 'Life of James Rogers', op. cit., vol. ii, pp. 442–3.
202 Ibid., pp. 466–7.
203 Hester Ann Rogers, op. cit., appendix pp. 242–3.
204 *JWJ*, vol. vii, p. 299.
205 *JWJ*, op. cit., vol. vii, p. 294.
206 Hester Ann Rogers, op. cit., p. 69.
207 *JWJ*, op. cit., vol. iii, p. 403.
208 Ibid., vol. vii, p. 76.
209 'Life of James Rogers' , op. cit., vol. ii, p. 467.
210 Ibid.
211 Hester Ann Rogers, op. cit., p. 69.
212 Ibid., Dr Thomas Coke funeral sermon, p. 208.
213.Hester Ann Rogers,op .cit., p. 69
214 *JWJ*, op. cit., vol. vii, p. 492.
215 Hester Ann Rogers, op. cit., pp. 69–70.
216 'Life of James Rogers', op. cit., p. 469.
217 *JWJ*, op. cit., vol. viii, p. 131.
218 Ibid.
219 Ibid.
220 Hester Ann Rogers, op. cit., pp. 7-11.
221 *JWJ.*, op. cit., vol. viii, p. 144. A pin containing the hair of
John Wesley, cut by Hester after his death, given to James
Rogers as one of the twelve preachers included in his will
to carry on the work of the Connexion, is now held by the
Wesley Chapel Museum in City Road, London.
222 'Life of James Rogers', op. cit., p. 469.
223 Ibid.
224 'Life of James Rogers', op. cit., p. 469.
225 Hester Ann Rogers, op. cit., Funeral Sermon, pp. 204–5.
226 Hester Ann Rogers, op. cit., p. 71.
227 'Life of James Rogers', pp. 470–1.
228 Hester Ann Rogers, op. cit., p. 71.
229 Ibid., Funeral Sermon, p. 205.
230 'Life of James Rogers', op. cit., vol. ii, p. 470.
231 Hester Ann Rogers, op. cit., pp. 205–6.
232 Hester Ann Rogers. Manuscript diary, op. cit., vol. 3,
p. 214.
233 Dr Thomas Coke Funeral sermon pp. 206–8

234 J,A,Hammerton, *An Outline of English Literature*, 1925, Educational Book Co. Ltd: London, p. 67.

235 'Life of James Rogers', vol. ii, p. 463.

236 J.A.Hammerton, op. cit., pp. 67–8.

237 'Catalogue of all the library books belonging to the late Thomas Legh Esquire of Adlington in the County of Cheshire,' 1830, J Needham Cliffe and Son: Macclesfield.

238 T. Pratt, The Portico Library, Manchester: its History and Associations, 1802–1922, Portico Library: Manchester, pp. 19–20.

239 Rev. George Whitfield, *The Age of Enlightenment, an Anthology*, S. Eliot and B. Stern (eds), 1979, Open University: Milton Keynes, p. 44.

240 Maldwyn Edwards, *Methodism and England*, 1944, Epworth Press: London, pp. 19–20.

241 E.H.Carter and R.A.F. Mears 'A History of Great Britain' ,Book iii, 1949, Oxford University Press, p. 698.

242 D.W.Bebbington *Evangelism in Modern Britain 1730s to the 1980s*, 1994, London Routledge p. 81.

243 *Methodist Hymn Book*, 1933 p. 156.

244 S. Eliot and B. Stern *The Age of Enlightenment: an anthology 1979*, Introduction to Vol I. Open University: Milton Keynes, p. vii.

245 Hester Ann Rogers, op, cit., p. 254.

246 T. Jackson (ed.), op. cit., p. 63.

247 J. Wolffe, op. cit., p. 41.

248 L. Davidoff and C. Hall, 'Ye are all one in Christ Jesus: men, women and religion', 1994, in *Evangelicals, Women and Community*, offspring collection. Open University: Milton Keynes, p.67.

249 Hester Ann Rogers, op. cit., p. 89.

250 Dr P. Mack, *Heart Religion in the British Enlightenment*, Cambridge University Press, 2008, p. 7.

251 Ibid.

252 J. Telford (ed.), *JWL*, vol. iii, p. 375.

253 Hester Ann Rogers, op. cit., p. 89.

254 Paul Wesley Chilcote, John Wesley as revealed by the Journal of Hester Ann Rogers, July 1775–October 1784, *Methodist History Journal*, vol. xx, part 3, April 1982.

255 Rosa E. Gladding, 'When Wesley came to Macclesfield, *Wesleyan Methodist Magazine*, February 1913, p. 133.
256 D.J. Bosch, *Transforming Mission,* 1996. Orbis Books: New York, p. 53.
257 D.J. Bosch, op. cit., p. 52.
258 Hugh Price Hughes, op. cit., p. 3.
259 Hugh Price Hughes, op. cit., p. 3 .
260 Rev. Thomas Champness, *Joyful News*, p. 1.
261 Hugh Price Hughes, op. cit., p. 3.
262 *Joyful News*, op. cit., p. 1.
263 D.W.Bebbington, 'The Holiness Movements in British and Canadian Methodism in the late Ninteenth Century', The Wesley Historical Society Lecture, 1996, p. 205.

Bibliography

William J. Abraham. *The Logic of Evangelism*. William B. Erdmans Publishing Company: Grand Rapids, 1996.

Catalogue of all the library books belonging to the late Thomas Legh of Adlington in the County of Cheshire: J. Needham Cliffe & Son, Macclesfield, Cheshire 1830

John Banks. *Nancy, Nancy*. Wilmslow Penwork Ltd: Leeds, 1984.

D.W. Bebbington. *Evangelicalism in Modern Britain*. Routledge: London, 1994.

D.W. Bebbington. *The Holiness Movement in British and Canadian Methodism in the late 19th century*. Wesley Historical Society Lecture, 1996.

D.J. Bosch. *Transforming Mission*. Orbis Books: New York, 1996.

Asa Briggs. *A Social History of England*. Weidenfeld & Nicholson: London, 1994.

R.W. Brunskill. *East Cheshire Textile Mills*. RCHME: London, 1993.

Vicki Tolar Burton. 'Re-reading *The Account of Hester Ann Rogers*', in *Angels and Impudent Women*, Norma Virgoe (ed.). Wesley Historical Society: Oxford, 2007.

E.H. Carter and R.A.F. Mears. *A History of Britain*, Book 3. Clarendon Press: Oxford, 1949.

W.H. Chaloner. *Lancashire and Cheshire Antiquarian Society*, vol. l, xii, 1950–1.

Thomas Champness. *Joyful News*. W.J. Tyne: Bacup, first edition, 1883.

Paul Wesley Chilcote. 'John Wesley as revealed by the journal of Hester Ann Rogers, July 1775–October 1784,' in *Methodist History Journal*. USA, vol. xx, part 3, April 1982.

Thomas Coke. Funeral sermon published in *Experience and Spiritual Letters of Hester Ann Roe*. T. Woolmer: London, 1885.

Nehemiah Curnock (ed.). *Journal of the Rev. John Wesley, AM.* Robert Culley: London, 1909.

Rupert E. Davies. *Methodism.* The Garden City Press: London, 1976.

C. Stella Davies. *A History of Macclesfield.* Manchester University Press, 1968.

L. Davidoff and C. Hall. *Evangelicals, Women and Community,* Offprints Collection. Open University: Milton Keynes, 1994.

J.B. Dyson. *A Brief History of the Rise and Progress of Wesleyan Methodism in the Leek Circuit.* Leek, 1853.

Maldwyn Edwards. *Methodism and England: A Study in Methodism in its Social and Political Aspects, 1850-1932.* Epworth Press: London, 1944.

S. Eliot and B. Stern. *The Age of Enlightenment: an anthology.* Open University: Milton Keynes, 1979.

G. Eliot. *Adam Bede.* Collins: London, 1859.

Charles Garrett. *Joyful News.* S.V. Partridge: London, 1883.

J. Gaulter. *Memoirs of the Rev David Simpson, MA, Minister of Christ Church, Macclesfield (1775-1799), friend of Wesley.* 1799.

Rosa E. Gladding. *Wesleyan Methodist Magazine.* February 1913.

K. Gnanakan. *Kingdom Concerns.* Inter-Varsity Press: Leicester, 1998.

J.A. Hammerton. *An Outline of English Literature.* Educational Book Co. Ltd: London, 1935.

David Hempton. *Evangelism in English and Irish Society, 1780-1840.* Oxford University Press.

H.P. Hughes. *Joyful News.* S.V. Partridge: London, 1883.

Janice Lynn Burton Jackson. *Not an Idle Man; A Biography of John Septimus Roe, Western Australia's First Surveyor General, 1797-1878.* Fremantle Arts Centre Press: Fremantle, 1982.

Thomas Jackson (ed,). *The Lives of the Early Methodist Preachers,* vol. ii: *The Life of James Rogers.* Tentmaker Publications: Stoke-on-Trent, republished 1998.

Bibliography

V. Kiernan. *Evangelism and the French Revolution*. Oxford University Press, 1952.

J. Lawson. *A Thousand Tongues*. Paternoster Press: Exeter, 1987.

C.F. Legh. *Adlington Hall*. English Life Publications: Derby, 1978.

C.F. Legh. *The Organ at Adlington*. H. Oldfield & Son Ltd: Macclesfield, 1978.

James C. Logan. *Theology and Evangelism in the Wesleyan Heritage*. Abingdon Press: Nashville, 1994.

Phyllis Mack. *Heart Religion in the British Enlightenment: Gender and Emotion in Early Methodism*. Cambridge University Press, 2008.

G. Malmgreen. *Silk Town: Industry and Culture in Macclesfield, 1750-1835*. Hull University Press, 1985.

C. Morison. *Macaulay*. London, 1882.

E.H. Nolan and E. Farr. *History of England*. vol. iii: 'From the Accession of George III. to the Twenty-Third Year of the Reign of Queen Victoria'. James S. Virtue: London, 1859.

G. Parsons. *Religion in Victorian Britain, Interpretations*, vol. iii. Manchester University Press, 1988.

J.C. Bowmer and J.A. Vickers (eds). *Letters of John Pawson*, vol. i. Methodist Publishing House: Peterborough, 1995.

T. Pratt. *The Portico Library, Manchester: Its History and Associations, 1802-1922*. The Portico Library: Manchester, (1922).

H.D. Rack. *Reasonable Enthusiast: John Wesley and the Rise of Methodism*. Epworth Press: London, 1992.

J. Ritson. *The Romance of Primitive Methodism*. Edward Dalton: London, 1909.

Hester Ann Rogers. *Experience and Spiritual Letters*. G.R. Sanderson: Toronto, 1885.

D. Rosman. 'Faith and Family Life', in *Evangelicals and Culture*. Croom Helm: London, 1984.

T. Shenton. *Forgotten Heroes of the Revival*. Day One Publications: Leominster, 2004.

Silk Heritage Group. *Bridge Street*. Friends of Macclesfield Silk Heritage, 1998.

144

David Simpson. *Sermons on Useful and Important Subjects.* T. Bayley: Macclesfield, 1774.

B. Smith. *History of Methodism in Macclesfield.* Pub. Unknown, 1875

Dorothy Bentley Smith. *A Georgian Gent and Co: The Life and Times of Charles Roe.* Landmark Publishing Ltd: Ashbourne, 1993.

Paul C. Smith. *Whatever happened to our Raison d'Etre*, Headway Conference Lecture, 1997.

A. Taylor. *Wesley's Chapel and Leysian Centre.*

John Telford (ed.). *The Letters of the Rev. John Wesley.* Epworth Press: London, 1931.

E.P. Thompson. *The Making of the English Working Class.* Victor Gollancz: London, 1968.

G.M. Trevelyan. *English Social History.* Longmans Green: London, 1947.

J.D. Walsh. *Evangelicals, Women and Community in 19th-century Britain*, 1992 Lecture.

J.D. Walsh. *Elie Halevy and the Birth of Methodism.* Tansactions of the Royal Historical Society: London, reprinted 1975.

D.L. Watson. *The Early Methodist Class Meeting.* Discipleship Resources: Nashville, 1985.

Wesleyan Methodist Magazine. 1824, 1857, January 1913.

J. Wolffe. *Evangelicals, Women and Community in 19th century Britain.* Open University Study Guide, Open University Press: Milton Keynes, 1994.

Andrew Worth. 'From Fame to Obscurity', in *Bulletin of the Wesley Historical Society*, London and Home Counties Branch, Spring 1993.